mibia

"For our children
ndrew and Sue Bannister
and Susie Johnson"

Peter Johnson (left) and Anthony Bannister have chosen a way of life in which their intimate knowledge and love of Nature can be fully expressed. As professional wildlife photographers they travel throughout the African subcontinent, preferring to focus their lenses on the scenery, wildlife and peoples as yet untouched by the forces of change. This quest for the spirit of wilderness has been combined with the realisation that man cannot be excluded from the picture and wherever they go, Johnson and Bannister help instil an understanding of the value of Africa's vanishing wildlife.

Previous books – their joint *Okavango: Sea of Land, Land of Water* (1977) and Johnson's *As Free as a Bird* (1976) – have received international acclaim and their photography is in constant worldwide demand.

AFRICA'S HARSH PARADISE
namibia

Anthony Bannister &Peter Johnson

DOMUS BOOKS
Chicago • New York

Compiled and edited by René Gordon

Hubert Berry contributed the material on Etosha. He has a distinguished academic record and world-wide experience as an entomologist in Africa, Spain, Greece, Turkey and the U.S.A. He is currently Chief Professional Officer at Etosha National Park where his work as a research biologist is focused particularly on the ecology of the blue wildebeest. As well as serving as an Honorary Consultant on the Survival Service Commission of the International Union for the Conservation of Nature, Switzerland, he serves on several committees for the preservation of wildlife. He is author or co-author of many scientific and popular articles and books on wildlife.

Dr K.F.R. Budack, consultant on the section dealing with the Nama, is an anthropologist whose main field of interest is the study of traditional Khoikhoi culture. His Ph.D. thesis was on the 'Traditional Political Structure of the Khoe-khoen in South-West Africa' and he has published a number of papers on the history, culture and oral tradition of the peoples of Namibia.

Alexander Colin Campbell contributed the Bushman material included in this book. His interesting career includes work for the Department of Tsetse and Trypanosomiasis and a degree in Sindebele. Since settling in Botswana he has conducted a population census (1964), researched and recorded customary law, become Director of the Department of Wildlife, and is now the founder-Director of the National Museum and Art Gallery at Gaborone. He has published widely, mainly on wildlife, but also on history, law and anthropology.

Eric Lloyd Williams wrote about diamonds and the diamond industry for this book. He has vast journalistic experience and has also written on a variety of other southern African subjects.

Dr J.S. Malan was consultant and contributor of material for the section on the Herero-speaking peoples of Kaokoland. An anthropologist, his first contact with Namibia was in 1968 when he began post-graduate research among the Herero-speaking peoples. His doctoral thesis was on the double-descent system of the Himba. In 1973 he was appointed ethnologist on the staff of the State Museum in Windhoek. He has also published extensively in *Cimbebasia*, a scientific journal of the Windhoek Museum. At present he is doing research on Owambo and Kaokoland.

Garth Owen-Smith was consultant and contributor of material on Kaokoland and its peoples. Trained as a forester, he was appointed Agricultural Supervisor for the Kaokoveld in 1968 where he made a study of land use in the territory. He spent a year in Australia as a research assistant and in 1973 returned to Namibia where he joined the State Museum, Windhoek, working with Dr J.S. Malan on the ethno-botany of Kaokoland. Subsequently he has been involved in conservation education programmes and is currently employed as an ecologist. His work has appeared in a variety of publications.

Dr Mary Seely contributed the material and was general consultant on the Namib Desert. Since she assumed the directorship in 1970 of the Desert Ecological Research Unit at Gobabeb in the Central Namib, Dr Seely and a small staff have co-ordinated all Namib research and conducted basic research into the desert ecology and related subjects. She is the author and co-author of both scientific and popular articles on aspects of Namib ecology and has assisted with several films in the field. Her principal research centres around the ecology of the Namib with special focus on fog water uptake by Namib tenebrionid beetles, ecophysiology of several dune plant species and bioenergetics of the Namib dune ecosystem.

Dr Peter Shaughnessy, consultant for the chapter on the Benguella Coast and the material on the Cape fur seal, is a geneticist by training and began specialising in seals during the course of an Australian National Research Expedition to Macquarrie Island in 1966. In 1970 he was offered a fellowship at the Institute of Arctic Biology at the University of Alaska where he completed his doctorate. Since 1973 he has been involved in intensive study of the Cape fur seal.

Professor Roy Siegfried acted as general consultant. He is the Director of the Percy FitzPatrick Institute of African Ornithology. His professional career has embraced marine, freshwater and terrestrial ecology and he has carried out original research in all these fields. He has been a visiting professor in the Department of Ecology and Behavioural Biology at the University of Minnesota and a research fellow in Canada and Europe.

Library of Congress Cataloging in Publication Data

Bannister, Anthony.
    Namibia : Africa's harsh paradise.

    1. Namibia - Description and travel - Views.
I. Johnson, Peter, joint author. II. Title.
DT703.B36   968.806   79-10312
ISBN 0-89196-060-0

First published in North America in 1979 by
Domus Books
400 Anthony Trail
Northbrook Il. 60062

Copyright photography © Anthony Bannister & Peter Johnson.
Copyright text © C. Struik Publishers (Pty) Ltd.

ISBN 0 89196 060 0

Printed in the Republic of South Africa

ACKNOWLEDGE-MENTS

Without the great deal of assistance we received from many organisations and individuals throughout the length and breadth of Namibia much of our photographic work would have been far more difficult if not impossible; the outstanding hospitality of the Namibians must be experienced to be believed. To all those who gave us help and encouragement we would like to express our very sincere thanks and we are particularly indebted to the following: Our wives, Maudanne and Claire, for their support at and from home while we were away for such long periods; the Director and his staff of the Department of Nature Conservation and Tourism for permission. and assistance enabling us to work in some of the magnificent parks under their administration; the Chairman, Directors and staff of De Beers Consolidated Mines Ltd and Consolidated Diamond Mines of South West Africa Ltd for their outstanding co-operation and enthusiasm; the Managing Director and staff of John Ovenstone Ltd for the many facilities they placed at our disposal at Walvis Bay; the Director and staff of the Desert Ecological Research Unit at Gobabeb for their friendly co-operation and advice; Suidwes Lugdiens and Etosha Fly-In Safaris for their efficient operations; and to the following individuals who gave so generously of themselves, their knowledge and their time:

Barbara Anderson, Sigi and Ann-Gret Eimbeck, Martha Gorski, Len and Marie Kloot, Mike and Sabena Krafft, Johannes Ruiter, the Springers, Brother Steiner, Johan and Ulna Steyn, Taishé, and Waitavira Tjambiru.

1. A shroud of life-giving fog steals inland across the Namib Desert.

2. Sand deadens the sound of hooves as oryx thunder across a dune valley in the southern Namib.

3. For over 160 kilometres the Fish River snakes its way through a canyon, almost menacing in its grandeur. In places the walls plunge over 700 metres to the riverbed where mud-curdled water flows fitfully to join the Orange River on its way to the sea.

4. Elements of the traditional Owambo way of life are translated into bold graphic forms from the air: the elaborately palisaded homestead, the brush-enclosed cattle kraal, the even furrows of freshly ploughed fields, the sandy well (top right) and the occasional wild fruit tree protected by taboo.

5. Along the coast, on the narrow sandspit dividing Sandwich Bay from the open sea, thousands of cormorants honour the territory of a handful of pelicans. The cormorants fish the rich green waters of the Benguella Current, the pelicans the protected environment of the lagoon.

AFRICA'S HARSH PARADISE
namibia

There is a stoic tenor to this landscape, to its people and its past. Essentially it is a desert land; along the entire Atlantic coast the Namib is parched and raw; to the east the Kalahari is harshly arid; along the central escarpment forbidding mountains rise like jumbled paleolithic hand-axes; the highlands give some respite; while the north can lavish water over a landscape sometimes green and sometimes aching with drought.

This is Namibia – for the undiscerning a place at best inhospitable: but for all who appreciate the unique, a singular world in every part of its existence – and in its future. Those who live here cherish their homeland, and consider it a gift for the chosen few. And there are very few; less than a million. Most are newcomers and only the Bushman and Bergdama can claim generation upon generation in this land. The Nama, the Portuguese, the Herero, the Caprivian, the German, the Mbanderu, the Afrikaner, the British – a veritable miscellany of mankind – have entered the Namibian arena within the last four hundred years.

If Africa's mythical cities and the fabled wealth of her monarchs had not been the constant dream of Europe's early cartographers, the history of southern Africa might have been very different. But Namibia's coastal profile offers no obvious charms and it is little wonder that the Portuguese chose to seek the legendary city of Vigiti Magna from the East Coast where they braved tropical forests instead of desert dunes guarded by a treacherous sea.

On Thursday, the 9th of November 1487, Vasco da Gama – and the Portuguese who followed him – concluded that the Benguella Coast of southern Africa was worthless, basing this on a crude survey of natural resources. Alvero Velho in his *Diario da Viagem* recorded the event:

'The Commander went ashore and showed them (the Nama) many goods to learn if there were those things in the land; and the goods were cinnamon and cloves and seed-pearl and gold and other things as well; and they did not know these things at all; and the Commander-in-Chief accordingly gave them little bells and rings of tin.'

There was no African Montezuma to be awed by the charge of a 16-horse troop of cavalry and the firing of muskets and cannon as on the beaches of Veracruz: the European adventure that began on the Spanish Main was not to be repeated in Africa at St Helena Bay.

The Portuguese found little here to inspire them, but others had already made this austere land their home. Long, long before either European or black man had felt the chill of the Namib's coastal fog, the Bushman had touched lightly upon the sands, accepting Nature's balance, at one with his environment. Nor had the diminutive Bergdama introduced clamour and discord to the desert silences, although he too had lived long in this land, a black race whose origins are unknown and whose culture has been lost like a drop in a turbulent ocean.

Only much later did the lowing of cattle presage the era of conflict that has dominated Namibian history for much of the past four centuries. From the south the Khoikhoi struggled over the hot sands, their herds casting dust-devils into the sky. And from the north the Herero came striding at the head of their herds in search of a land of their own, where their cattle would grow fat and numerous. The land that awaited them was not generous, for the greater part of Namibia is at best a marginal habitat for man and beast and competition over its sparse resources was a dominant feature of the early relationships between the Nama and Herero.

The Owambo, warlike people settled in the relatively well-watered and fertile north, largely escaped the internecine turmoil for they would tolerate no invaders. So, while the Owambo tended their millet and their women sang as they dipped their fishing baskets into the flood waters, the Nama and Herero plotted against one another and bartered their cattle for firearms with the traders at the coast. Of course there were then, as now, interested parties at the ringside – and in the middle of the arena, too. The 'Oorlam' tribes and others like them brought to Namibia an expertise and sophistication that added a further dimension to the basic Nama-Herero conflict. They well knew that the gun could be a decisive factor in battle and they must also have been fully aware that to ally themselves with the local Nama would earn them title to the new land.

Just as interested from another point of view were the coastal traders whose ships came loaded with liquor and firearms and departed with beef and hides. Germany's imperial thrust and Britain's colonial ambitions reached here, too, and eventually the outside world came to discern that beyond the fog-shrouded treachery of the coastline lay undreamt-of riches.

From the mid-19th century these new contenders had joined the fray, complicating the issues and increasing the bloodshed. If there is discord now it is an echo of the earlier forces of competition between herdsman and herdsman, but the new prize glitters in the crumpled rock and the sea-washed sands and the antagonists dream dreams of wealth and power.

Yet man is a very small figure against the sheer scale of the Namibian landscape and the human voice has done little to shatter its silence. Much of the land is untouched, the natural forces as yet unexplored.

This book is not an encyclopaedic view. The lens roamed free and wide, inspired like the text by the miracles of the landscape. If the choice of words and photographs seems arbitrary, it has nonetheless been true to a central theme – the natural splendour of this land.

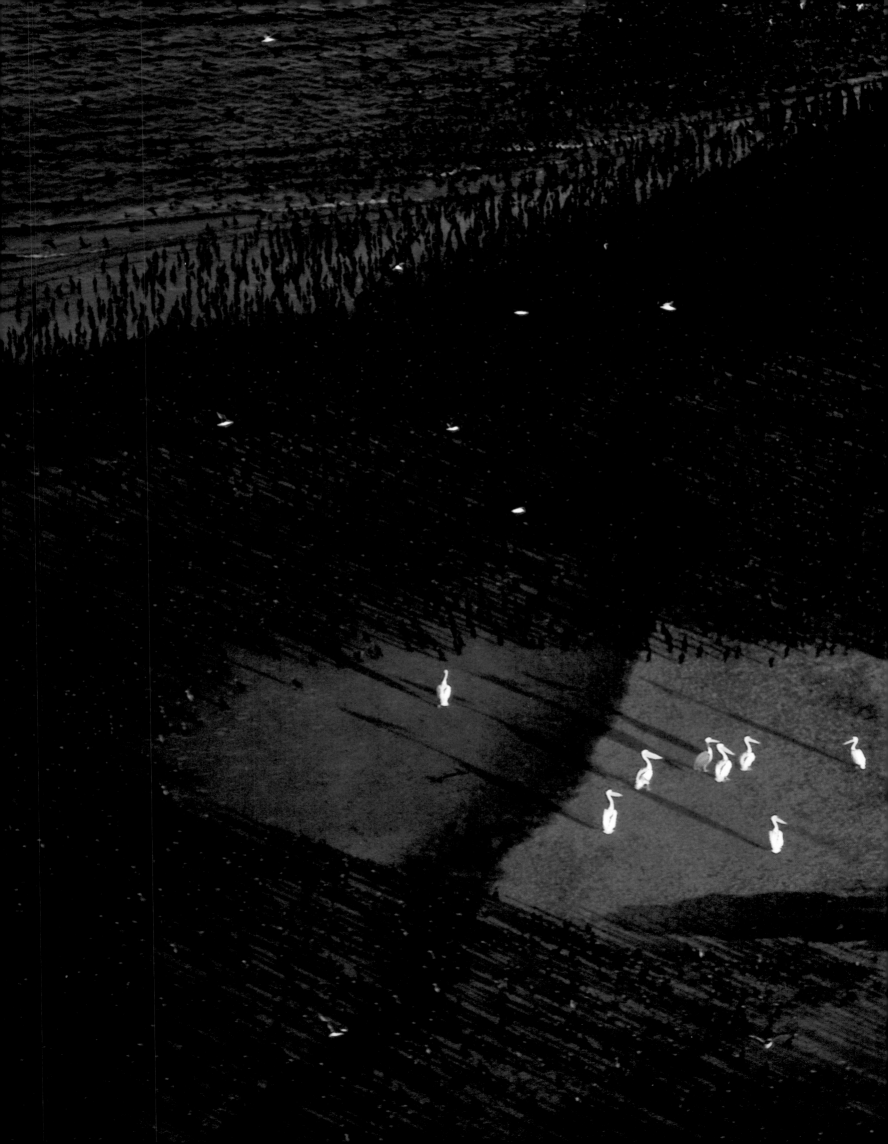

LAND OF CHANGELESS CHANGE

From an orbiting satellite the configurations of the Namib Desert dunes are as distinctive as the 'canals' of Mars. Neat parallel fingers of sand extend north and south for 300 kilometres, from the centrally situated riverbed of the Kuiseb to the equally dry Koichab, in an almost continuous sea of sand. Farther south, reaching to the Orange River, is another well-defined dune sea, and still others pattern the Namib, clearly separating desert dune from desert plain, dull orange sand from pale calcrete and gravel. Less than half the entire area is duneland; sometimes large islands of shifting sand, sometimes isolated pockets piled behind rocky outcrops or in riverbeds; and between and beyond are the contrasting tones of the level interdune valleys and featureless desert plains. In its entirety the desert stretches from Moçamedes in Angola to the Olifants River in South Africa. But, from an orbital vantage point, the most dramatic feature of this coastal desert is the incisive rôle of the Kuiseb River which effectively demarcates the limits of the slow northward march of the southern dunelands from the grey monotony of the northern gravel plains.

It is a land of changeless change, of unanswered questions; a desert unlike any other, unlike the Sahara, the Atacama, the Arabian or Baja. Here, each island of sand, whether the east face or the west, whether seaward slope or lee, is a microcosm, a little world – part of a larger whole yet supporting its own complex of animal and plant life. Not only do the beetles, the gerbils and the lizards, the plants and the insects of the windward slope differ from those of the slipface, not only do the creatures of the dunes differ from those of the desert plains, but the creatures of the Namib differ from those anywhere else upon this earth.

There is no certainty, but it would seem that the cold currents of this coast have been its constant companion for aeons and the winds that blow incessantly now, blew then too. 'Soo-oop-wa' the Nama call the perpetually moaning and sighing winds of the dune seas. For countless centuries they have blown, modelling the sands into their characteristic linear form. But the endless serried dunes, at a distance simple in structure, are in fact topped by a complex array of ridges, hollows, and cliffs of cascading sand or slipfaces.

The slipfaces are ever-changing, ever-moving. They are also the most important habitat of the seemingly barren desert wastes. Whichever way the wind blows, so the slipface, as if seeking refuge, moves to the opposite side. If the wind suddenly gusts from a new direction, the slipface too may change direction just as suddenly. It may even disappear altogether for a time – only to reappear under the influence of another wind. And sometimes, along the coast where the wind blows more constantly in one direction, transverse dunes, like sandy extensions of the ocean's waves, ripple along the coast.

But the winds are far more than just the sculptors of the Namib Desert. For part of the year a hot dry wind blows from the east. It brings no moisture; its burden is food for the creatures that inhabit this strange landscape: particles of organic matter which it distributes over the interdune valleys as a 'larder' from which the desert fauna can draw. At other times, the northwester, charged with moisture, comes in from the sea and lays a chill shroud of fog over the desert, providing the only regular form of precipitation to slake the desert's thirst. Very rarely, perhaps once in a decade or so, the sea winds may bestow their meagre showers. Then hidden rivers rise briefly to the surface, only to disappear within hours. The duneland is once more bleak and arid,

and nothing can be heard but the booming of the rollers against the desolate shore.

The dunes, the fog, the easterly winds; such are the vital factors on which life in the Namib depends. There are other cool coastal deserts – Chile's Atacama cooled by the Humboldt Current, California's Baja – where these same three elements are found, congruent factors that logic demands should create parallel phenomena. Yet only in the Namib has an endemic fauna and flora evolved in the vegetationless dunes. Perhaps because of its millennia of stability this desert has been a laboratory in which a highly specialised biota has been able to evolve. As vital might be the relative isolation of the large dune seas, surrounded by arid plains. Rain never falls in the Namib to the extent that grasses and shrubs from inland can bridge the plains and valleys and take hold and overrun the dunes. Neither can the larger predators gain a base in these inhospitable conditions.

The life of this desert has the stage to itself.

At the Namib Research Institute at Gobabeb in the southern dune sea, scientists of many disciplines try to unravel the desert's mysteries, to fathom the way of the winds now and in the past, to understand how this desert came to be. Yet Nature remains aloof, for she does not part willingly with her secrets. 'Soo-oop-wa' moans mockingly across the dunes, and man plods on attempting to explain the hitherto inexplicable.

THE LIVING DESERT As dense early morning fog rolls over the Namib dunes, a beetle little larger than a thumbnail stands motionless, its body elevated into the wind. And as it waits on a sandy ridge, droplets of water begin to coalesce on its poised body. Then slowly this flows along the insect's grooved back to its mouth. We have witnessed a miracle of the Namib – the *Onymacris unguicularis,* in one of the most bizarre adaptations to the extremes of this desert, drawing moisture directly from the fog.

For perhaps one day in five, fog bathes the Namib for some 50 kilometres inland from the coast, creating a cool 'fog zone' which sustains a complexity of plant and animal life uniquely adapted to utilise these minute amounts of moisture in the form of fog or dew droplets that precipitate on plants, on the sand, even on the creatures themselves. Such lifeforms are the primary consumers in the desert for not only do they 'drink' from the air, but many feed on detritus dispersed by the wind. Animals and insects unable to draw directly on these sources feed on those that do and so a biota entirely confined to the dunes has evolved.

The resources on which this biota depends are extremely marginal – rain rarely falls and when there is no fog to shroud the dunes the daytime heat can be oppressive. The wind blows often, sometimes this way, sometimes that, and the sands are ever restless. Only its unpredictability is certain: that is its paradox. Given this, survival in the Namib depends on flexibility – the ability to maximise on any set of advantageous circumstances, if and when they arise, and to simply avoid those that are not.

Escape becomes vital. Later in the day, when the fog has lifted and the sands are scorched by the sun, our tiny beetle rests in the cool depths of the sand, awaiting the evening when it will venture once more to the surface, this time to the base of the slipface to feed on detritus scattered by the wind. In the total silence of the midday landscape the only sound is the pulse of blood as it clamours through one's ears. Nothing stirs. Most of the creatures of the desert have escaped the heat by digging between 30 and 50 centimetres into the sand where temperatures vary only a few degrees during the year. Some doze in burrows scrabbled into the firm soil around the root-clumps of plants. The only other living thing we see out in the open is a lone oryx, torpid with heat, on the crest of a dune where cooling breezes may blow. For this great antelope there is no respite from the heat, nor is there any relief in perspiring and losing precious moisture. Alone on the dune crest, this large desert mammal simply tolerates the heat, its huge body absorbing it to the point at which its blood temperature is so high it would destroy the animal's brain were the blood not first cooled by circulating through a network of capillaries in the oryx's nostrils.

In the years when rain falls, the pale grasses toss their feathery seedheads in the wind and herds of up to 100 oryx graze deep in the dunes, drawing moisture from tiny underground tubers and, perhaps like the ostrich, even taking in condensed droplets of fog or dew from plants. But the oryx, just as the birds and black-backed jackal, the Cape fox and the hare, has an option – it can move out of the dune seas to the better-grassed and watered Pro-Namib that shimmers towards the distant foothills of the Great Escarpment.

The true fascination of this desert lies with the creatures which do not have this option: locked in the desert dunes they cannot survive elsewhere. Of the many lifeforms now known to live totally within the desert's confines the first to draw attention to the phenomenon of a dune-specific biota was the tenebrionid beetle, known over much of southern Africa as the familiar 'tok-tokkie'. Some 30 years ago a white-backed tenebrionid was discovered exclusively in the northern dune sea, separated from the southern by the Kuiseb River and some 200 kilometres of gravel plain. Its presence in only one part of the desert posed certain questions regarding the development and interrelationships of the various dune fields.

There are a multitude of species of tenebrionid in the Namib and this seemingly commonplace beetle has become the focus of exciting study. In analysing the past, the occurrence of the same species in now distantly separated areas of the dunes may help us understand events in the desert where there is little else of an organic nature on which to base modern methods of dating analysis.

But for the natural scientist the tenebrionid beetles of the Namib are even more intriguing. They do not differ much in appearance from those elsewhere – some are better-equipped to scramble over the loose sand of the slipface and in some the normally black wing-case is coloured white or sandy red or yellow. The main characteristics that set the desert tenebrionid apart from its other cousins are all behavioural adaptations. The 50 or so desert species have come to share the few resources of their habitat with a minimum of overlap and all are able to 'swim' to safety beneath the hot desert sands.

At the same time of day when our tiny *Onymacris unguicularis* moves slow and cold to the top of the foggy dunes, other tenebrionids are also out, although this is not their normal feeding hour. At the low temperatures of early morning they would still normally be under the sand waiting for the sun to warm the surface. But when by some

7. While the crest of this 'star' dune displays the complex array of ridges, hollows and slipfaces that are continually coaxed this way and that by the winds, its base, anchored by a light mantle of vegetation, is relatively stable. The dominant dune form is, however, linear and a spectacular example is shown on the previous page. Dunes such as this run for hundreds of kilometres south of the Kuiseb River, their margins blending into the parallel 'dune streets' of calcrete covered with a dusting of desert sand.
8. Vivid late-afternoon cloud brings a rare desert shower, but evaporation prevented a single drop reaching the ground.

8

little-understood mechanism they detect the fog, they leave the sandy depths. Some struggle slowly down the slipface in search of vegetation from which to drink the drops of fog and dew. Others search among dried tufts of grass and pads of detritus on which dew precipitates.

Just as remarkable is a small 'flying saucer' shaped species of tenebrionid which can extract moisture from between the grains of sand. When the fog is heavy this beetle begins to construct a trench that can be a metre in length, and is often placed perpendicular to the direction of the wind on the slipface or along the top of a ripple of sand. As the beetle forces its way through the top layer of sand it creates parallel ridges on which the fog strikes and precipitates so that these ridges soon contain two to three times as much water as the surrounding sand. Now the beetle retraces its path along the trench extracting the accumulated moisture as it goes, in the process demolishing the trench. In the laboratory any doubt is removed by the fact that these beetles, by drawing water

directly from between grains of wet sand, increase their body-weight by 30%.

Some beetles use one method exclusively, others appear to use two or more depending on circumstances – in other words they exhibit the flexibility needed to succeed in their desert environment.

In terms of the ratio of energy expended to benefit gained, this water-gathering may be wasteful and all the more questionable in a beetle that seemingly can do without. But perhaps the beetle, like so many of the living things of the desert, requires water to better ensure successful reproduction or enhance over-all activity.

In this environment characterized by scarcity of life-giving factors, water is the most scarce of all. It may not rain for years, but when it does, the gentle touch awakens seeds lying dormant between grains of sand, wedged between stones or locked in mud-crazed washes. The fog may sustain but it is the rain that brings the flush of new life to the Namib.

Plants no less than the other living things of this desert must be flexible to survive. The dunes know no seasons, but whatever the time of year, when 10 to 15 millimetres of rain fall at one time seeds germinate and the stark slopes are cloaked in green. Some will grace the sands but briefly, maturing within days and setting hundreds of seeds in the wind before withering away. Some seed will endure to quicken with the rain at another time and in another place, but most will be eaten by the creatures whose myriad tracks delicately pattern the sand each morning before the wind sweeps the only visible evidence of their existence from the surface.

Until very recently the Namib golden mole was known to exist by its tracks alone. On calm mornings the characteristic raised ridges with a slight depression between, traces paths between clumps of grass. Sometimes the tunnelling tracks change as the tiny mole scampers briefly over the surface before plunging into the sands once more to search for small

reptiles such as the legless lizard or beetle larvae which are the main items consumed by this voracious insectivore. The first clue to its true identity came from analysis of owl pellets which were found to contain the skulls of the golden mole. It exists, it has even been photographed, yet like so many things of this desert, very little is known about it.

Owls are among the few birds to enter the Namib. Most predators – both of the sky and on the ground – hunt among the dunes when the desert is in benign mood. After rain, the Namib is fecund. Perennial plants take on a flush of green and the plants and creatures that ensure survival by a shortened lifespan in the adult form are suddenly active. Later when the seeds and larvae are safely buried in the sand, the predators withdraw, leaving the sere landscape to those creatures that know no alternative existence.

In the apparent bleakness of the Namib questions as numerous as the grains of sand await answers. Early, before the sun arcs high, and again at sunset and in the night, the

Namib is alive. As the afternoon wind whips across the sands small yellow circular beetles are out, snatching bits of detritus from the air. The big black scorpion stalks its prey in darkness, and in the morning light a Ludwig's bustard skirts the dunes in search of tenebrionids on which to feed.

The *Aporosaura* lizard in the heat of the day performs a strange dance to regulate its body temperature. Lifting first one leg and then the other, it eventually becomes poised with opposite fore and hind legs arched high in the air together with its tail. We watch entranced for several minutes before the lizard, suddenly afraid, dives into the loose sand of the slipface and is completely lost to sight – another half-understood chapter in the story of the Namib.

There are termites and strange spiders, rare plants and bright red scarabs, snakes and scorpions, beetles and nocturnal reptiles, web-footed lizards and desert larks: so far scientists have sketched the plot only in broadest outline, they have identified some of the characters and integrated some of the scenes, but the masterwork will be a long time yet in the writing.

9. Strange lizard of the Namib, the almost transparent palmatogecko emerges at night to hunt. Its delicately webbed feet may increase stealth but more probably help it burrow into the dunes and escape the daytime heat.
10. Entranced by its aggressively stylised display when threatened, early scientists called this spider 'the dancing white lady'. Its method of flight, however, is even more spectacular: it folds its legs inwards and using the momentum of its body, cartwheels down the slipface or dune slope. Another smaller spider folds its legs in similar fashion to be blown to safety by the wind. Apart from such behavioural sequences little is known of these desert spiders. The body juices of a hapless cricket make a meal for this lady.

11. Many of the creatures peculiar to these desert dunes are able to draw moisture directly from the fog and feed on windblown detritus: others, unable to utilise these resources, must prey off those that do. Here ants *(Camponotus detritus)* suck up moisture from the fog which has precipitated on the stem of a !Nara plant and run down onto the sand.

12. Sensitive whiskers and quivering nostrils alert for danger, a gerbil ventures from its daytime hideaway.

13. Another nocturnal creature of the desert, the rarely seen and even more rarely photographed Namib golden mole, surfaces briefly before resuming its 'swim' through the sand in search of food. This small insectivore has only rudimentary eyes and depends on super-sensitive hearing to seek its prey.

14. When on the surface in the heat of the day the *Aporosaura* lizard performs an intriguing thermo-regulatory dance, lifting first one leg and then another clear of the sand and eventually becoming poised in an outlandish arabesque with opposite fore and hind legs raised and tail arched high in the air.

15. In three deserts continents apart – the Gobi, the Baja and the Namib – are snakes which have all evolved the sidewinding method of moving over a loosely compacted and often hot surface: the identical solution to a similar problem. They gain maximum traction yet limit body-contact with the surface, leaving distinctive tracks as they go. To hunt, the Namib's sidewinding Peringueyi adder conceals itself in the sand and only its eyes, set high on its head, reveal its presence.

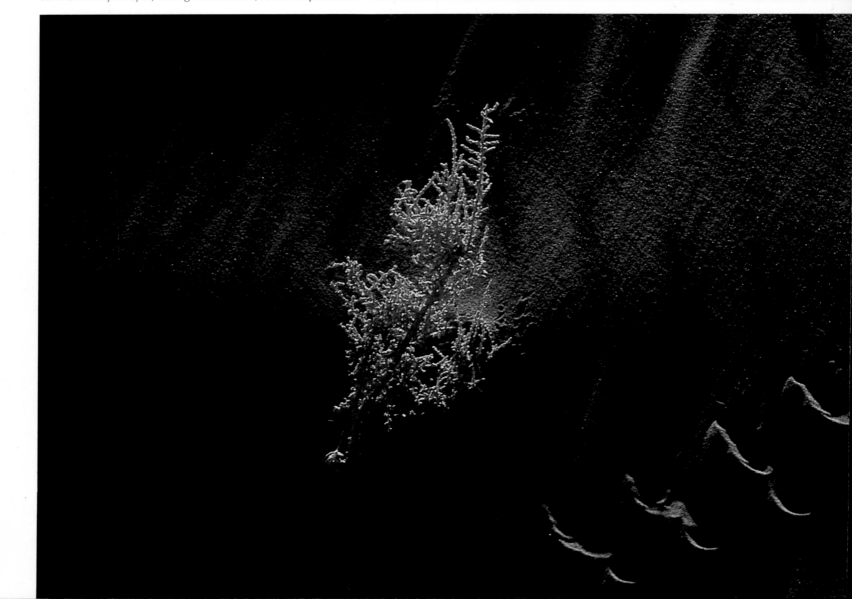

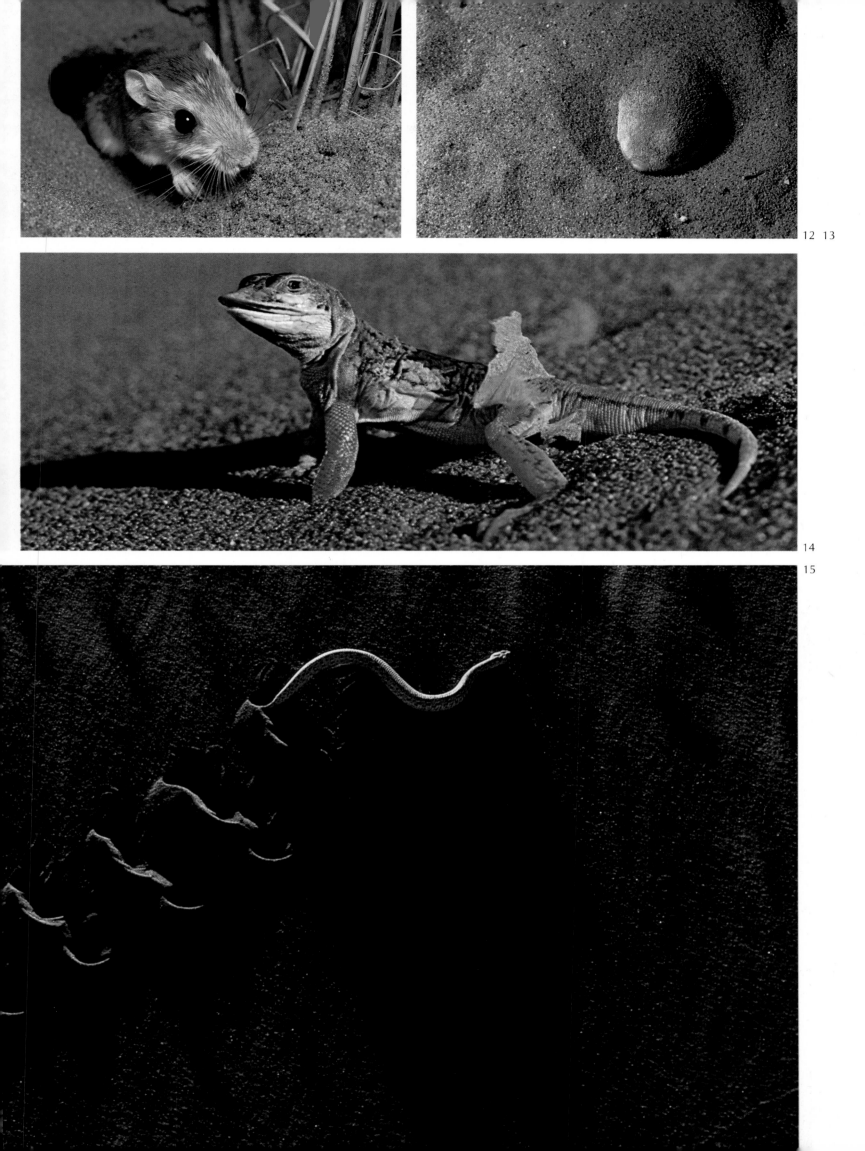

12 13

14

15

16. Lifting fog reveals the Namib. The explorer Charles Andersson wrote in 1873: 'Indeed it might vie with the Great Sahara in sterility and dreariness; and the weary eye seems to range in vain over this howling wilderness in search of some object worthy of attention.' But his description is unduly bleak: the Namib is relatively benign, for the cold Benguella Current moderates the temperatures of this coastal desert, and the clammy sea mist that rolls over it one day in five at once protects it from the sun and bestows precious moisture for the unique fauna and flora which have evolved here.

17. Droplets shimmer on desert grass after heavy morning fog.
18-21. As fog settles over the dunes an *Onymacris unguicularis* emerges from the sanctuary of the sandy depths where temperatures vary little throughout the year (18). Cold and slow, the beetle moves to the top of a ridge and elevates its body into the wind. Now moisture begins to coalesce on its limbs and body (19) until the liquid rolls forward to its mouth (20). In one of the most bizarre adaptations to this desert environment, the *Onymacris* beetle 'drinks from the air' before retreating underground once more (21).

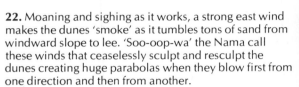

22. Moaning and sighing as it works, a strong east wind makes the dunes 'smoke' as it tumbles tons of sand from windward slope to lee. 'Soo-oop-wa' the Nama call these winds that ceaselessly sculpt and resculpt the dunes creating huge parabolas when they blow first from one direction and then from another.

23. Exposed and sandblasted, this !Nara root as thick as a man's thigh once penetrated deep underground to reach water. The plant adaptations of the Namib are as marvellous as those of its animal and insect world. After rain the *Stipagrostis* grasses, tall and stark here, develop fine feathery heads of tiny aerodynamic seeds which may be carried 100 kilometres or more by the wind. Once their journey has ended the awns detach and the seeds lie dormant until a rare shower of rain triggers germination.

24. The freak rains of 1976 brought a flush of plant-life to parts of the Namib that had long lain barren. Within a fortnight the grasses set seed – evidence of the ability of desert plants to germinate and mature quickly whenever good conditions may by chance prevail.

25. The dunes at Sossusvlei, probably the highest in the world, tower 300 metres or more into a pale desert sky.

26. For centuries after Diego Cão first sailed into Sandwich Bay in 1486 it offered safe harbour to traders and smugglers, explorers and settlers. But gradually the sea and sand asserted their dominance. Today a sandspit partially divides the ocean (in the background) from the reed-fringed lagoon. Sweet water seeping from beneath the dunes sustains the green surround which is a breeding ground for the diversity of animal life in what is now, by Nature's own decree, a sanctuary for creatures which might otherwise find this a hostile coast.
27. Against a backdrop of dunes, pelicans fly low over the lagoon.
28. Reflections at Sandwich Bay.
29. Flamingoes scramble from the surface at Sandwich Bay.

27
26 28

THE COAST OF LONELINESS

Only a few kilometres inland along Namibia's desert coastline are ancient lagoon beds lined with prehistoric white mussels the size of a man's hand (31). In the heart of a coastal dunefield, light suffuses a delicate microlith (32) discarded by Stone Age people who dwelt along the banks of a river long dry. Today the wind reveals the rivercourse, tomorrow the smothering sands may move on and there will be nothing until another wind in another era brings sunlight once more to these fragile tools of forgotten men. In 1909 the *Eduard Bohlen* was stranded on the Skeleton Coast (30). Today she rests a kilometre from the present shore, her superstructure wallowing in a sea of sand. In time, like the ancient galleon uncovered by diamond prospectors far inland, she may be completely engulfed by the dunes that march inexorably into the sea.

Sailors have always been wary of this changing coastline that makes charts unreliable all too soon. Entombed within the shifting sands are the skeletons of men and ships, testimony to the desert's intolerance of living things. Yet this desert coast itself seems a living, creeping thing. The sands edge grain by windswept grain seaward, broadening the beaches, encroaching on the waves.

There was a time, thousands of years ago, when antelope browsed the shrubs along green riverbanks and hunters with rough-hewn weapons stalked their prey. Perhaps the rainfall on the highlands was greater and the rivers which end abruptly at places like Sossus Vlei and Tsondab Vlei burst through to the sea. But now the desert is master and the sweet waters ripple and fade mid-course beneath the dunes.

There is evidence of more recent occupation; the middens of the Khoikhoi who sojourned at the coast when the interior was gripped in drought – but even they rarely retrace the ancient routes to these dreaded shores. The only people who venture here now do so equipped to face the fury of the 'coast of loneliness', and immediately their business is done they leave the barren landscape to the moaning winds, the shifting sands and the bleaching bones of those who did not pay their due respects.

30
31 32

WELWITSCHIA: *Native of the gravel plains.* Friedrich Welwitsch crouched on his knees on the Namib's hot desert plains on September 3, 1859 and stared in bewilderment at what he recognised to be one of Africa's most inconceivable creations – the *Welwitschia mirabilis;* a plant that bears his name and even now, more than a hundred years later, is but partly understood.

Mirabilis – Latin for marvellous – well suits this plant. According to some estimates certain of these gnarled ancients that squat in apparent disarray on the desert floor today, were in existence as long ago as the birth of Christ. They have endured as the single species of a singular genus, part related to the cone-bearing pine and part to flowering plants.

Large but scattered communities dominate the solitude of the northern Namib desert wastes. Like a monstrous turnip, a metre in height above the ground and thrust no more than three deep, the Welwitschia endures in timeless tolerance. Around each plant is a tangle of dessicated leaf-tissue shredded by centuries of wind, scorched by constant sun, and apparently sustained by the fog. The tangle is but two – a pair of thick olive-green straplike leaves that grow in never-ending conveyor-belt fashion from the woody central core. Only the newest growth is green, but zebra, springbuck and oryx occasionally chew at the tough leaves, and the snaggled mass is an important microhabitat. Fog settles heavily on the leaves where it can be used by other living things, but how the host itself utilises this water is still unknown. The nutritious seeds are a source of food for the creatures of the desert and the Welwitschia sets many, although the majority are infertile or diseased. Carried northwards by the prevailing winds, the seeds that survive the hungry herbivores, disease and heat wait patiently for sufficient rain to trigger growth. Then the seed strikes root, quickly establishing itself. So effective is this method that some believe there may be a direct correlation between the age of successful stands of 'young' Welwitschia and meteorological records of particularly good rains in the Namib. At such times ephemeral plants grace the desert – succulents and bulbs blossom and grow fat. The few hardy perennials grow apace. As the drought sets in again most of the plants disappear. The ephemeral grasses die off, leaving their legacy of seed. The bulbs hide in the soil, leaving no sign of their existence above ground. Some plants roll up their leaves or wither on the surface. And the *Welwitschia mirabilis* is once more alone.

33. The tree-lined bed of the Kuiseb River clearly limits the northward creep of the pale orange Namib dunes from the grey monotony of the northern desert's gravel plains. Although the Kuiseb may flow no more than a few days each year, its rush of water has an incisive rôle in clearing away the accumulation of sand seen encroaching here on the windblasted Hamilton Range. But the dunes are relentless and have managed to race ahead at the coast, entirely blocking the Kuiseb's exit to the sea and forcing its waters beneath the sands.

34. Ancient *Welwitschia mirabilis* squat among their disarray of tattered leaf on the Welwitschia Flats near Swakopmund. This arid wash may well be the point of origin for these strange plants over which the pioneer naturalist Friedrich Welwitsch in 1859 exclaimed: 'I am convinced that what I have seen is the most beautiful and majestic (creation) that tropical southern Africa can offer.'
The main distribution of the plant fans north and east of the Flats which suggests that the prevailing south-westerly winds of the Namib have been a major factor in the dispersal of the Welwitschia. As it is, very few of the seeds which this plant sets are germinable and even those that are not diseased are likely to be eaten long before rain provides the trigger for the seeds to set root. However, seeds capable of withstanding years of drought are but one of the many other seemingly miraculous adaptations by which the plants of the Namib ensure survival in their almost waterless habitat.
35. Lurking among the flowers of a male Welwitschia plant, this well-camouflaged crab spider catches a nectar-seeking fly.

36

37

38

9

0

36. End of a successful hunt for this scorpion on the northern gravel plains.
37. A nocturnal gecko veiled by its partially moulted skin.
38. *Mesembryanthemum cryptanthum,* a fleshy-leaf succulent of the gravel plains of the Namib north of the Kuiseb River.
39. The 'ice plant', so-called because of the large water-filled cells which cover leaves and stem.
40. Like a string of living beads, the *Psilocaulon* lies moisture-filled on the hard-baked floor of a desert wash.
41. What is the selective advantage of being white? This is but one of the many unanswered questions relating to the white-backed tenebrionid beetle. Here the smaller male shades the female with his body, allowing her to forage longer on the surface.

41

THE MEN OF MEN Across the plains near Gibeon dust puffs into the parched air as a mounted commando scuffles and skirmishes in mock-battle with historic foes. The riders wear distinctive insignia: brightly coloured sashes across their chests, hats draped in white cloth and embellished with bold cockades.

For two days each year the Witbooi tribe of Khoikhoi gather here to relive in dusty pageant the great victories of their past. For the Witboois themselves it is an affirmation of their place in history as fighting men, but in the broader context of the Khoikhoi it has more sombre overtones as a final mustering of a people who once followed long-established migratory routes throughout southern Africa, from the Kunene River in the north to the Kei in the east and south to the Cape of Good Hope. Indeed the 42 000 Khoikhoi, who live largely in Namibia and call themselves Nama, are the remnants of a proud people with a long history on the subcontinent.

At Gibeon the people cluster beneath a few great trees in the corner of the graveyard to hear stories of their heroes, men such as Hendrik Witbooi who challenged the Germans and Herero less than a century ago. And the stories that are told during those hot October days are part of an ancient oral tradition that tells of creation and the genesis of their people. The Witboois look to their recent history, but the Khoikhoi as a whole can look to older heroes of whom the greatest is Heitsi Eibib who led his followers westwards towards the setting sun until their wanderings brought them to the Atlantic and there, so tradition has it, he founded the Khoikhoi – 'the men of men'.

He was born to a virgin mother who swallowed the sap of magic grasses – a creation myth that springs from the fountainhead of man's collective unconscious. But from here the legendry of Heitsi Eibib is African: he is always portrayed as the possessor of cattle as numerous as the blades of grass – the Khoi ideal of happiness and success. In the mythology of his people he is endowed with supernatural powers that allow him to change shape at will, pass through rivers and mountains, and like an African Phoenix die many times only to rise again. In the past no Khoikhoi would pass one of Heitsi Eibib's graves without placing another stone upon the cairn and perhaps uttering this prayer for good luck:

Oh Heitsi Eibib
Thou our grandfather
Let me be lucky
Give me game
Let me find honey and roots
That I may bless thee again
Art thou not our grandfather
Thou Heitsi Eibib!

The choice of phrase is surprising for the Khoikhoi are a pastoral people; yet much that they celebrate in their rich and diverse literal tradition – success in the hunt, in the search for honey and edible roots – could just as easily belong to that other honey-coloured people of the southern continent, the Bushman.

There are many similarities between the Khoikhoi and the Bushman (whom the Khoikhoi call San – hence the widely used term 'Khoisan' when speaking of both) and early voyagers who met these slight people along the coast did not differentiate between them. Admittedly they are very similar physically. Both, unlike the dark-skinned Bantu-speaking peoples, have a rich apricot-coloured complexion, slender, delicately modelled hands and feet, heart-shaped faces with prominent cheekbones, and tapering chins. Their full lips are slightly everted as if poised to kiss. One of the early chroniclers described their hair as 'like the wool of lambs' and their eyes as 'beautifully black and as clear and pure as those of the hawk'. The epicanthic fold of the upper eyelid and almond shape of the eye gave rise to the belief, now disproved by geneticists, that the Khoisan were an outflung tribe of the Mongolian people.

Adding to the earlier confusion were the 'clicks' so characteristic of both Khoikhoi and Bushman tongues. One account written in 1595 described their speech 'as if one were to hear some turkey cocks making a noise . . . of which little else can be heard than a clucking and whistling'. To the unaccustomed European ear the beautifully modulated yet staccato tones of the Khoisan tongues were incomprehensible and the Hollanders at the Cape called the Khoikhoi *Hüttentots*, meaning 'stammerers'. Gradually this changed to 'Hottentot', a term used until quite recently when it took on derogatory overtones and fell into disfavour.

In early eye-witness accounts of the Khoikhoi there is a strange omission – perhaps the result of a certain 'delicacy' in regard to such matters among the early chroniclers – not one refers to the unusual accumulation of fat on the buttocks, the steatopygia so admired by the Khoikhoi, particularly in their women.

It fell to the anthropologists and ethnographers to define the differences between the various peoples and in the final analysis these were found to be mainly cultural and linguistic. It is possible that the Khoikhoi are descended from a mixture of Bushman and later pastoral invaders, the Hamitic-speaking peoples who moved south from equatorial and north-east Africa bringing the longhorn cattle and fat-tailed sheep that came to be associated with the Khoikhoi. Even more intriguing is the possibility of origins in Tanzania where to this day at Sandawe there is a click language that shares many root and grammatical likenesses with the Khoikhoi tongues.

In Namibia three basic divisions of Khoikhoi can be discerned. One grouping is the Namen who have probably lived along Africa's Benguella Coast for several hundred years, moving between the waterholes of this arid region and in years of extreme drought following traditional routes to the sea where they lived on fish and seafood until rain fell and they could return inland. All along this wasteland coast are ancient middens littered with mussel shells and fish bones left by the so-called 'Strandlopers'. Only recently was the myth of a lost race of beachcombers disproved and the Khoikhoi identified as the people who ate the fish and danced around the campfires while the Atlantic rollers boomed against the shore.

Then, some 180 years ago, the 'Oorlam' clans moved across the Orange River from what is now South Africa. They were largely remnants of southern Khoikhoi, some of whom had interbred with the Dutch settlers at the Cape and acquired a degree of sophistication that was to be a marked advantage in the subsequent conflict first with the Herero and then with the Germans. Among these people were tribes who to this day bear names which reflect the strongly patriarchal nature of Khoikhoi society: the Witboois and Afrikaners, for

42. A Topnaar settlement huddles on the stark northern bank of the Kuiseb River. Goats are the main symbol of wealth and, now that hunting is prohibited in this area, milk is the main source of nutrition. The dark stains of undecomposed goat droppings near the homesteads are evidence of the aridity of this region. The acacias in the foreground grow on the desert sands which impinge on the river from the south.

instance, are named after the strong charismatic leaders from whom they are descended.

During the bloody years of turmoil when herdsman clashed with herdsman and Herero and Khoikhoi disputed rights to waterholes and sweet grazing, the official reports are filled with other names as well – the Topnaars, the Groot Doden (Great Dead), the Red Nation of Hoachanas and the Velskoendraers (those who wear shoes).

In the classification of the Namibian Khoikhoi there is a third group, included because they speak a Khoi dialect and show some traits of Khoi culture, but in fact they are more closely allied to the Bushman.

The Khoikhoi are a displaced people. When the Europeans settled at the Cape of Good Hope and turned their eyes to the pastures inland, the Khoikhoi could either assimilate or retreat. Those who chose to withdraw met the hostile Bantu-speaking peoples to the east. After losing many people and cattle, the Khoikhoi turned north where they became embroiled in battle against the already beleaguered Bushman. And so, pursued on all sides, the survivors bent their hopes towards the west, to Namaqualand, to the thirstlands of the North West Cape and, finally, to Namibia.

Their culture straddled the values of the patriarchal pastoralist and of the hunter-gatherer. While cattle were the ultimate source of wealth and status, the link with the past and the guarantee of the future, the Khoikhoi also looked to hunting and the plants of the veld for sustenance. In their endless search for grazing they had no need to build permanent structures. They set up their beehive-shaped huts of layers of rush matting laid over a light frame within the protection of an encircling thornbush fence. The huts were arranged clan by clan, the individual doorways always facing east – the direction from which Heitsi Eibib is said to have come long ago. At night the cattle, sheep and goats were close-kraaled in the centre of the encampment and when pasture and water grew scarce the huts were dismantled and loaded onto oxen. Then the people mounted their riding oxen and driving the pack-oxen before them set out to seek better conditions elsewhere.

The beehive reed hut is so ideally suited to Namibian conditions that even some whites in the southern reaches of the country and Namaqualand have adopted it, for in summer the rushes shrink in the heat and air circulates freely through the interior, whilst in winter they swell, providing a water-tight cocoon.

Today the Khoikhoi are a mere shadow of their former selves, numerically and culturally. Three centuries of war have cost many lives but have also provided sweet moments of victory which still inspire some of the clans, despite inroads on their identity from all sides.

The Witboois who gather for their annual festival at Gibeon arrive in panel vans and motor cars, not on pack-oxen; and when the celebration is over they return not to kraals filled with cattle as numerous as 'blades of grass', but to white-owned farms, dusty towns and scattered homesteads round distant waterholes.

At Hoachanas there are remnants of the Red Nation, at Warmbaths there are Bondelswarts, and in the star-filled nights at Sesfontein the Topnaars still make music as their ancestors did. Sometimes when the moon lifts the shadows in the mountain clefts one hears like distant bells the reed flutes, each tuned to produce a different note but played by an ensemble. Gradually, as one listens, the flutes are drowned out by the high-pitched voices of the women as they sway and thrust their hips and clap their hands in time to the soft sweet music. At other times the stirring words of praise poems ring in the night.

A rich legacy of proverbs and riddles, folk tales and poetry has been handed down from generation to generation. These lines from the recently recorded 'Praise of the Red Nation' are a fine example:

> You who are difficult to tame
> Valiant eye
> Generous one who is often scolded
> Big camelthorn with many branches . . .

The Khoikhoi have intermarried with the black man and the white, they have adopted the best and the worst of western civilisation, yet in powerful words such as these a proud cultural tradition endures.

43. Namib dunes hulk large behind the riverine fringe of acacias as a Topnaar family trundles home along the Kuiseb.

44-49. Early each year many Topnaar make expeditions to harvest the !Nara melons which grow in the dunes along the Kuiseb River near Walvis Bay. It is a time-consuming and arduous task. Each is prodded for ripeness and then teased from the patch with a stick (44). After the harvest the sweet-tasting pulp, which has a strong herbal smell, is removed (45) and boiled over a fire (46). The seeds are strained from the 'soup' and the cooked !Nara is poured onto clean sand (47). After two or three days the pancake is turned so that the oil from the other side can drain away. When dry, it is cut into strips and eaten as a sweet which is placed against the palate and licked rather than chewed because of the sand adhering to it. The seeds are dried in the sun (49) and most are sold to dealers in Walvis Bay who export them as a delicacy. Among the Topnaar 'shop food' has become a sign of status but the poignant words of the praise poem on the following page convey something of the !Nara's significance in former times.

PRAISE POEM TO THE !NARA MELON

You round food
With many thorns
You many-breasted
Foster mother of the Topnaar children
Even if I am far away
I will think of you
You food of my ancestors
I will never forget you

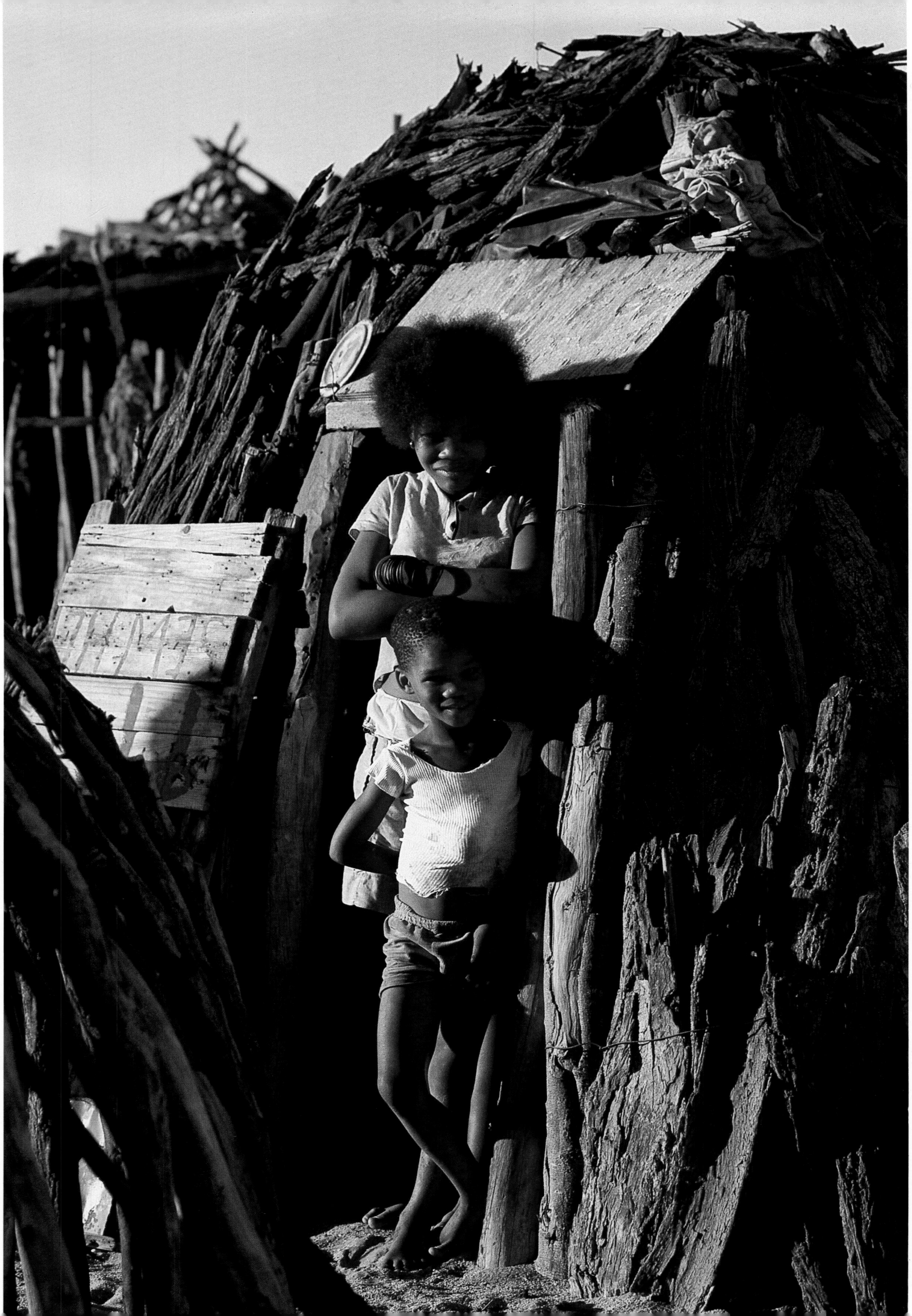

50. Few Nama still build these traditional huts of acacia bark; corrugated iron is preferred today.
51. Gert Swartbooi, whose distinctive features reflect the Khoikhoi ancestry of the Nama people, was born at Klipneus along the Kuiseb and the river is still the anchor in his life. Hidden in its sandy depths is the water that sustains his goats, his chickens and his children; and keeps his small garden alive. The acacias provide the material from which his home is built, fodder for his flocks and, when the larder is empty, something to fill the stomachs of his family.
52. Moonrise over the Namib gravel plains near Ganab.

53

54

56

55

53. Animals, such as these springbuck, trekked into the desert from surrounding areas after the unprecedented rains of 1976 transformed the Namib wastes into open grassland.
54. Kokerboom *(Aloe dichotoma)* thrust their thick sappy trunks among the boulder-strewn terrain of the Kokerboom Forest near Keetmanshoop. Early travellers observed how the Bushmen used the fibrous core to make quivers and it is still widely known as the 'quiver tree'.
55. In the Skeleton Coast Park a lone euphorbia overlooks a landscape of stony desolation.
56. Oryx grazing on the Namib gravel plains below the Heinrichsberg.

57. In their hundreds these Namaqua sandgrouse glided down to drink briefly at a pool in the Namib. Many of the male birds (one shown in flight) waded in to soak their specially modified breast feathers before flying off. By means of this remarkable behavioural and structural adaptation they carry water, often many kilometres into the desert, to the chicks which nibble at the saturated feathers, releasing the water and drinking at the same time.
58. Nocturnal, shy and solitary, a strandwolf lopes across the desert as evening falls. In the Sperrgebiet, an immense expanse of 'forbidden territory' that isolates the diamond mining area, the brown hyaena (strandwolf) finds sanctuary. It scavenges the great rookeries of Cape fur seals and in its lonely ramblings along this melancholy coast, feeds on what the sea may toss ashore.
59. Ostrich flounce across a sere plain in the Sperrgebiet.

60. A pale swathe of sand between harsh mountains marks the Swakop River, and its tributary the Kahn, in which water seldom flows on the surface but courses in considerable quantities underground. Early travellers journeying into the interior would inspan their wagons at the river mouth at Swakopmund and then follow its well-defined path upstream as far as Otjimbingwe, confident that by digging down into the sand, water could always be found. Today there are plans to utilise this flow on a large scale and provide water for schemes such as the nearby Rössing Uranium Mine.

61. The Tinkas Mountains, part of the escarpment which runs like a rugged spine parallel to the coast along the entire length of the country.

62. An aloe of heroic proportions in the Pro-Namib.
63. A charmingly grouped family portrait of rock hyraxes (dassies). Nearest relative of these furry
little creatures is the elephant.
64. Closely hugging the distant escarpment, the Pro-Namib forms the better-watered margin
between coastal desert and highlands. Grass and clumps of euphorbia enhance this view inland of
Luderitz.

65
66

65. Talons firmly embedded in its prey, a martial eagle strokes with powerful wings as it lifts a hyrax from a rocky slope.
66. A Nama shepherd drives his flock across the Pro-Namib, where karakul farming has become the basis of a highly lucrative industry. One of the oldest breeds of domesticated sheep, the karakul has transplanted successfully from the steppes of central Asia to the thirstlands of Namibia, where it was introduced, via Germany, in 1907. At birth the karakul lamb's pelt is smooth, dark and marked with the rippling wavelets of curls for which it is so admired.

67. It was several months since rain had fallen here yet this natural pool in the highlands was still deep and clean. Watering-places such as this are vital to the wildlife of the escarpment but no creature disturbed this image of the distant Pondok Mountains reflected on its mirror surface.
68. Incongruous in the arid highlands, tadpoles dart in the remnants of a mountain stream.
69. As this pool evaporated so its green cloak of algae flourished, creating a luxuriant cape for this seemingly bemused bullfrog.
70. Through a magnificent natural rock arch some 50 metres long, the Pondok Mountains seem to float, dreamlike in the distance.

67 68

69

LANDSCAPES OF THE SOUL

LANDSCAPES OF THE SOUL The Abbé Breuil, pioneer student of African rock art, suggested the motivation for the thousands of pictures with which early man adorned the rockfaces and cave walls of southern Africa: he called them simply 'landscapes of the soul'.

Twyfelfontein is a magnificent site of rock engravings (more accurately petroglyphs). It lies just north of the Brandberg, and here the men who painstakingly chipped the designs and beautiful animal pictures fully expressed their artistic urge.

During the many millenia since the first artists began to decorate the rocks at Twyfelfontein, time has laid a fine patina over their creations. The oldest have weathered to the same reddish-black of the mother-rock, the more recent stand out pale and clear. With picture superimposed upon picture the evolving styles and the development of rock art in this area can be traced; yet it is all but impossible so far to date accurately the earliest.

Quite as intriguing as the question of age is the question: Who were the early artists of Twyfelfontein? Many were doubtless ancestors of the present Bushmen and Nama, but some of these fine engravings could well have been the work of the Bergdama, a short, stocky negroid people whose origins are obscure and whose cultural identity has been lost.

Of the few examples shown here, the engraving of an eland at Twyfelfontein (71) embodies certain techniques and a style typical of some of the art in the area; for instance the animal is shown in profile with spoor instead of feet. A work of particular lyricism and power is the central figure of a lion (73) from the 'lion slab'. One can only wonder whether the spoor attached jauntily to the animal's tail is no more than a delightfully humorous endnote.

These early hunters also decorated other sites along Namibia's rocky escarpment with paintings and engravings; and the giraffes (72) in white and earthy tones in the Etemba cave, high up in the Erongo Mountains are examples of their work.

Although we are not always certain of the identity of the artists, one fact is without dispute: the rock artists of southern Africa were producing paintings here at the same time as, if not earlier than, the famous rock artists of Altamira and Lascaux in Europe.

73

74. A pale mist swirls about the massive Brandberg Mountains which soar to over 2 500 metres – the highest point in the country.

71 72

THOSE WHO CAME FIRST

Less than a million people live in Namibia; of these fewer than 15 000 are Bushmen and no more than 2 000 still live as we have recorded them here. As hunter-gatherers they will soon disappear leaving no trace of their going for their touch upon this earth is so light that the bush will simply crowd a little closer about the forgotten campsites and the nut shells and ostrich egg fragments will slowly settle into the soil. Only the Bushman's oxide-rich paintings and deft engravings on rock faces and outcrops – and his many stone tools – will recall the thousands of years when his was the only human figure in the southern African landscape.

To find Bushmen living in the traditional way is a rare experience. Alec Campbell still recalls his first impression of an encampment: 'It was set back about a kilometre from a dry pan. In all it consisted of seven shelters – little more than branches dug into the ground, their ends bent over and plaited into a roof and covered roughly with tussocks of grass. A few flat-topped acacias gave straggly shade. There was not a blade of green; no rain had fallen for several months and the harsh October sun baked down onto the bare sand. The ground was littered with nut shells and a few embers smoked listlessly before the open entrance of one shelter. This was !Gole, a place I had travelled over 350 exhausting kilometres through scrub and bush and along endless sand tracks to find. I was totally bewildered by the apparent desolation.

'A man rose from the shade of a tree, lumps of sand peeling from his back and thighs. Apart from a skin drawn between his legs and tied around his waist, he was naked. Now other mounds of sand moved, broke up and revealed figures: an old woman, a young one and two children. My eyes turned to the bushes hung with a few skins tanned and scraped clean of hair, a small grass mat, a skin bag containing a quiver full of arrows and a bow. In the shadows at the back of one of the shelters were some ostrich eggs gleaming like pale moons. Several swollen tubers and an enamel bowl, old and chipped and filled with seeds, lay beside a dead fire. An iron pot, one of its three legs broken off, lay on its side amid a pile of melon rinds. Otherwise there was nothing, nothing at all except the heat and the silence and the five people rising from the sand.'

This was one of the last places in southern Africa where Bushmen still lived in the traditional way, hunting wild animals and collecting plant food. After that encounter in the early 60s, Campbell was to see many encampments but the image of that first one remained deeply etched in his memory – the harsh environment, the apparent poverty and the figures rising from the sand. And over the years, like so many people who have been privileged to observe the Bushman's way of life, he came to realise that while on the material level he seems to have nothing, the Bushman in fact has something of infinite value – an unshakable sense of belonging. From birth he knows who he is, his place in the greater order of things, and that he need never be alone.

The resting figures at !Gole had remained at the camp while the other members of the band went to collect the meat of a giraffe which had finally been killed after a gruelling five-day hunt. The old woman was ill and her daughter-in-law stayed behind with her two children to look after her. During the intense heat of the day they lay in the shade and covered their bodies with sand well-saturated with urine to keep cool.

The remainder of the band came back that night. Campbell describes their return: 'They could be heard long before they could be seen, their song

thrusting back the evening as they staggered through the darkness, even the smallest carrying a load of meat. A ululation, rising and falling, was taken up and thrown from person to person, each coming in on a different key yet harmonising beautifully; a wordless song that rose and fell, quickening in beat until it trailed away as they came into the edge of the firelight.'

In all there were 14 people camped at !Gole, a tiny band in the immensity of the Kalahari Desert. Lost in this monotony of sand and scrub and sky the outsider immediately feels the chilling fear of isolation. But the Bushman does not share this fear. His territory is as familiar to him as the streets are to a city dweller. He does not see desolation about him – every bird and caterpillar, springhare and oryx, each tangled bush and lonely baobab is a co-citizen in his world.

The Bushmen have a fund of stories and beliefs which explain their position in the environment. They have the same right to exist as the plants and the animals, the clouds and the rain for all are neighbours. The Bushman takes what he needs, no more, and Nature replenishes the common fund; if he should violate this natural order, the moon, the sun, the wind and the rain will bring drought, sickness, disease and death.

According to Bushman mythology there was a time long, long ago when all the animals were people, when strange things happened which no longer occur, a time when the trickster God, Kauha, lived with us on earth. This was the time of the beginning when God was a mere mortal, the time before he went into the skies and became divine: a period when time stood still, when life was different yet the same. One set of stories about this magical time revolves entirely around Kauha and his family who are constantly playing practical jokes on one another. Megan Biesele, who studied the mythology of the !Kung Bushmen, found in the many tales centred on Kauha's daughter-in-law significant elements relating to the Bushman's attitudes towards the balance of power between the sexes, marriage, birth, blood vengeance and the all-important sharing of meat. Kauha himself is the pivotal figure in stories that explore the fundamentals of living – hunting, food collecting and so on.

A second group of stories, peopled by a great variety of characters, deals with many themes including creation and death.

The !Kung story of the division of the social world into hunter-gatherers and herder-cultivators is particularly revealing. Megan Biesele translates: 'We who were made first, have come to be last. And those who were created last have come to be first. Even though they arrived later than we did, Europeans and Bantus have come to be ahead of us.'

Kara#túma, a Bushman ancestor, is blamed for the fact that the black man learnt to plant crops and herd cattle while the Bushman did not. In the story explaining these events Kara#túma was the first to see cattle but he did not appreciate the significance of the tame beasts. Instead, he showed them to the black man who realised their significance and became a herdsman. The black man's knowledge of agriculture is similarly explained. But while the Bushman shows dissatisfaction over this, he also displays a fatalistic acceptance of the world as it is, rather than as a place that can be actively changed.

As one Bushman put it: 'I refuse this thing that we should have come to be the last of all . . . It gives me pain. And I despise that old man of long ago who caused it to happen. I think if I saw him today I would beat him. But he's dead and there's nothing that can be done.'

The mythological era ended, so the Bushmen claim, when man became separate from the animal world. They say: 'Before this we were all people together, but after this we were divided each to his own.'

Although these fables and tales relate to the !Kung, the largest group of Bushmen living in Namibia today, they are common to all Bushmen. At night beneath the immensity of the desert sky the people often cluster round the fires to listen to the old people tell stories. The audience is spellbound, repeating a phrase now and then, or shrieking with laughter at some particularly bawdy event or devious ploy. They do not take the content seriously and will often finish a tale by saying: 'My goodness, the way people behaved in the old days was amazing!'

For years it was believed that the Bushman was physiologically adapted to his harsh environment, but this is only partly true. Unlike the oryx he cannot tolerate a drastic rise in body temperature, nor does he sweat less than we do. His ability to live in the desert is to a large extent the result of cultural rather than physiological adaptation.

Everything is shared, from the discomfort of the September heat to the bite of the cold desert winds in May. Accepting his world for what it is, the Bushman knows that after the heat of the day must come the cool of the evening and after the drought must come the rains.

The Bushman's survival depends on an incredible knowledge of his environment. He knows when and where every food plant will grow and as a result wastes little time and effort on random searching over the veld. He knows the habits of the birds and the beasts that share his territory – he even knows when he can safely drive a lion from a kill and take its meat or when it is best left alone. All this knowledge is gained through experience; there is no formal teaching. Each person learns of life through living.

Among the Bushman living as hunter-gatherers there is little innovation; things are still done in fundamentally the same way as they have been for generations, yet there is also flexibility. Nowhere is this more dramatically demonstrated than in the annual splitting up of bands who live in areas where the waterholes dry up for several months at a time. Then, when the rains fall and there is plenty, these groups come together once more at their traditional waterholes. Yet, in areas where there are waterholes which can be depended upon throughout the year, the bands tend to congregate during the dry season and then disperse after the rains.

As archaeologists lay bare ancient campsites it becomes evident that the Bushman's way of life has endured for as many as 20 000 years. It appears, too, that with the exception of iron which has replaced stone, and pottery which was introduced later, the material culture of the hunter-gatherer has remained largely the same over the last 10 000 years. Once the Bushman inhabited almost every part of southern Africa: some in fact suggest that he evolved here. Today he is largely confined to the more desolate areas of the Kalahari wastelands and it is likely that his way of life – apparently simple but in fact highly complex – which took thousands of years to evolve will within the next few decades disappear completely. Only his genetic imprint will remain: short, delicate stature, apricot-coloured skin and peppercorn hair.

About 4 000 years ago the Khoikhoi entered southern Africa and much later still the black man migrated south, bringing his cattle and his iron technology. Finally the European made his presence felt. All these had a considerable effect on the Bushman who either retreated, usually into the mountains, or was absorbed. It is unlikely however that he

was, as so often portrayed, 'pushed before the advancing horde', for wherever the Bushman has been studied he appears to have a culture so well adapted to his environment that it could only have developed through prolonged experience.

It is becoming increasingly difficult to distinguish traditional culture. Even the Dzu/wa (part of the !Kung), who are the only Bushmen in Namibia still living a hunter-gatherer existence, have been considerably affected by contact with surrounding peoples.

The Dzu/wa live in small bands within a territory, splitting up, moving around and then converging again, depending on the availability of edible plants and surface water. Their territory contains few waterholes that can be counted on during the long dry months from March to November: seldom more than shallow wells dug in dry riverbeds or small springs, but vital. Each belongs to a band or a number of bands whose members have a right to use it. Similar rights extend to staple plant foods, and although the Dzu/wa cannot explain exactly how these rights came about, there is no doubt among themselves as to who may collect where, and who may drink from a particular waterhole.

The system works so well that there are few squabbles over anyone's rights, but at the same time it is flexible enough to permit very general movement; and band visiting by individuals and families is a common occurrence. But these movements are by no means haphazard, and this is essential to any understanding of the Bushman's way of life: there is nothing haphazard about it; everything is carefully though not consciously planned.

When a band decides to move, the decision – which is always by consensus – is based on a vast and profound knowledge of the natural resources available. And it is this that helps them survive in an environment where others would surely perish.

The women, carrying their babies slung in karosses, set out each morning to collect wild foods. They always know exactly where they are going and regulate their time of departure accordingly. If the distance is great, say ten kilometres, they leave at first light and begin collecting as soon as they arrive, before it becomes too hot. If they are to spend the entire day out in the veld, and they know that there is no water where they are going, they carry it with them in ostrich eggs, baobab fruits or in bags made from the innards of animals. During the heat of the day they rest, but if food is

76. About them the landscape stretches in apparent monotony, but for Nisa and Kanha every part of it is familiar. Armed with no more than their digging sticks and an intimate knowledge of their environment they will soon fill their karosses with nuts, berries and tubers.

extremely scarce they may collect a little more in the afternoon before returning to camp. If there are old people in the band the children stay with them in the camp; but the older ones may sometimes accompany their mothers.

Plant foods grow in specific areas and in communities. For instance, if the women are looking for truffles they look in areas of hard soil, pan floors and old riverbeds, not on the summits of dunes.

The !Kung are able to name about 250 plants of which they actually eat about 100. Richard Lee in his research noted that only nine species are of major importance and one of these may form about 50% of the diet of some Bushmen. It is not that they prefer the taste of these plants; it is simply that they are the easiest to collect and have the most reliable regeneration.

By far the most sought after is the *mongongo*. This tree (*Ricinodendron rautanenii*) which normally grows in groves in sandy areas has a soft fruit with a hard nut containing an oily kernel. The Bushmen make expeditions to these groves well into the dry season for they know that although the flesh may rot from the nut as it lies on the ground, the hard shell will protect the kernel.

No band's territory contains all the most important food plants, but each contains either *mongongo* or the other major food plant, the *tsi* bean (*Tylosema esculenta*, more commonly known as *morama* or the gemsbuck bean).

Although the Bushmen deliberately make use of certain plants which they consider vital, they collect all the others, but do not go out of their way to do so. They can always fall back on a wide variety because during years that are bad for some species, there are always others available. Even in the worst years when drought grips the land, they are able to survive by being widely selective.

Only when they hunt large game do the Bushmen expend considerable time and effort on an uncertain result. Meat is relatively unimportant to the Dzu/wa as a source of food – most of their food is vegetable – but the sharing of meat is a vital cohesive factor in their social life and it is for this reason above all that the men stalk the large mammals of the desert.

Sharing is the basis of Bushman survival. It means much

more than simply sharing things; it means sharing activities, experiences, health and sickness, hopes and fears. No one goes off by himself without telling the others. He may go hunting alone, but he will have discussed it in case others wish to accompany him. And even if no one joins him he may borrow an arrow so that his hunt is symbolically shared. A man's arrow is very personal to him, almost an extension of his hunting arm, and by using it another hunter borrows some of his skill and a measure of his hunting luck.

Hunting large animals requires the co-operation of two to four men. Years of careful observation have taught the Bushmen a great deal about their prey. They know, for

77. One of the first attempts to introduce the Bushman to a settled life was at Tsumkwe in the heart of Bushmanland. Today, 20 years later, it is a settlement of some several thousand !Kung Bushmen whose grass shelters surround the school, well, clinic and trading store. Here they live in a state of flux, neither cultivators nor herders yet increasingly reluctant to return to their traditional way of life.
78. Dam, only 11 months old and barely able to see over the grass, plays all day long with the older children, keeping up with them; in this he reflects the typical early development of Bushman children.

example, where kudu tend to feed, to rest up during the day and to move in the evening. From tracks they can tell male from female, wounded from unwounded. Often they can tell where an animal is wounded, how badly and how long it is likely to travel before the poison takes effect.

In the early 1960s Campbell hunted with three Bushmen in the Okwa area. He recalls how they set out in the early afternoon. 'If we go in the morning we will not be able to shoot until evening, so let's go now when we need not be in the sun all day,' they said. We walked north, scanning the ground for fresh tracks. It is not often that you see game in this setting before you see its spoor and, besides, the Bushmen like to study the tracks to see how the animals are moving before they make contact with them. This allows them to work out the herd composition, whether they are moving far or just feeding, travelling into the wind or with it – all important factors in this open landscape where the kill is difficult.

We soon found fresh tracks – about four hours old, to judge from the trampled grass and the state of the animals' droppings. The hunters estimated that there were seven oryx

moving slowly with the wind and feeding on melons. 'If we follow directly they will scent us,' said G//au. 'We will go round and hide in the bush near a big melon crop which is not far in front.'

We moved fast, often running for a kilometre or two, until we approached the melon patch from the north. G//au was right: the oryx were already feeding. We crouched in the bushes discussing in whispers which animal should be hunted. 'Not the pregnant one, it will run far to save its baby, nor the old bull, it will also fight to live.' The final choice was a sleek young male. 'It is used to being chased from the herd by the older bulls; when the poison starts working it will not struggle to keep up with the others.'

We huddled under the bushes until late afternoon. Now two hunters moved to the west and rapidly approached the herd, coming out of the sun so that the oryx were blinded. Bending almost double, they used every possible cover, at the same time watching the Bushman who had remained with me and who kept signalling what the animals were doing. When he indicated that they were disturbed, the hunters froze; when the oryx lowered their heads to feed once more the

hunters shuffled forward as fast as they could. When they were about 20 metres away the oryx took fright and ran. Almost simultaneously each man released an arrow aiming for the stomach and, even before this found its mark, fitted another arrow to the string and fired again. Then they were off, running like the oryx themselves, until hunters and hunted were out of sight.

'They will follow until the wounded one breaks from the herd; then they will examine its tracks so that we can find it tomorrow. Now it is nearly dark and soon the oryx will become dizzy from the poison and stand still. If we leave it all night it will not be able to run when we find it tomorrow.'

Once more he was correct. Next morning just as the sun lifted above the horizon we picked up the tracks and within an hour found the wounded oryx lying in the open. It staggered to its feet as we approached but it was too far gone to run and the Bushmen rushed in with their spears for the kill.

The carcase was cut up in the veld and every able-bodied person in the encampment came to carry home the meat. Now began the sharing that is so basic to the Bushman way of

life. The 'owners' of the waterhole divided up the meat and each person knew what his share should be. The hunter or the owner of the arrow which killed the animal received one part, his brothers another and so on. Each person who received meat divided it again among his relatives and hunting associates. Everyone received a share and eventually everyone had roughly the same amount of meat.

Another important aspect of sharing is the giving of gifts. The actual items involved vary from group to group. The !Kung women, for instance, make very beautiful jewellery from ostrich egg-shell, which they wear for some time before giving it away to a friend or relative, in the knowledge that eventually they will receive a gift in return. Such gift-giving within the band cements bonds and helps control envy and potentially hostile emotions. A man with a fine iron pot will not keep it for long; soon one of his relatives will admire it and he will give it away without expecting anything in return, knowing that if he sees something he admires he need only say so and eventually it will be given to him.

The exchange of gifts also establishes relationships with other bands, even those living far away. Gifts pave the way to marriage and create bonds not only between the giver and receiver, but between the people who accompany the gift and those of the receiver's band. Once a person marries, he or she has rights in the territory of the spouse's band. Thus people with no *mongongo* nuts in their territory can always visit relatives who have plenty of this food in theirs and join the other band in collecting them.

The open voicing of criticism is another way of dealing with potential conflict. A man or woman with a grudge will express their feelings in a monotone which the band recognises. In the tiny huddle of shelters everyone hears but they know that these are just thoughts and they do not appear to take notice. What is more, no one may take offence. This allows people to let off steam while communicating criticism in a socially acceptable way.

Probably the greatest yet least known ritual of the Bushman is the trance dance. In the past all men took part in these dances and many achieved a state of trance; but as alien cultures make their presence felt, so the art has become more specialised and fewer men can do so. The dances were practised regularly and sometimes as often as twice or three times a week the special fire was lighted.

Campbell describes one of them: 'The women sit in the glow of the fire and a few begin to clap and sing. Others soon join in and the tempo quickens. Suddenly a man rises and starts to dance, his heels smacking into the sand as he shuffles slowly around the fire. Another joins him and the women ululate louder and faster, new voices joining in at different levels and throwing the chant back and forth across the fire. One feels a mystic presence as the glorious voices of the women well up and fill the desert night. Another man rises and joins the dancers, holding the man in front of him at the hips. Dance follows dance and dancer follows dancer and the atmosphere is charged with tension until the men, singly or in pairs, go into a trance.

Sweat pours from them and they turn, placing their hands upon and around individual singing women. Eventually they collapse onto the ground where they lie unconscious until their companions pick them up and walk them around and they regain their senses. I have seen men in deep trance seize burning coals from the fire and rub them over their chests and armpits. Sometimes they try to throw themselves into the fire but are thrust away by the women or others taking part. The dances often continue through the night, some men going into a trance ten or more times until the dawn signals another day.'

The Bushmen believe that while in the state of trance they are able to absorb and remove sickness from others, particularly women. This serves a dual purpose for it establishes the dependence of women on men and at the same time sets the Bushman's world in the greater world of the unknown.

Today there are no Bushmen who have not seen white people and no areas where an alien culture has not been felt. Even among the Dzu/wa these changes will in time cast aside their age-old culture. Their way of life which over thousands of years found equilibrium – that rare achievement which eludes modern man – will not equip them to live in our world when theirs is irrevocably lost.

79. Nisa scrabbles deep in the dry earth for a large bulb she has uncovered with her digging stick. Her efforts are rewarded: roasted, it will help feed her family. In general, the gathering of wild plants by the Bushman women makes a larger contribution to the family cooking pot than the hunting expeditions of the men.
80. Kumsa and Qui search for fresh spoor in the forested dunes of the northern Kalahari.

81-88. Xau digs beneath a glossy-leaved commiphora and sifts the sand through his fingers (81) to find the chrysalids of *Diamphidia* beetles whose body juices will provide the deadly poison for his arrows. These apparently insignificant grubs (82) contain toxins to which there is no known antidote and which can kill a man within hours. He carries them home in a bird's nest (83). In a pestle made from an eland's knee-cap he mixes the poison compound made of a powdered red bean (84), the juices of a *Diamphidia* grub (85) and the sticky juice of a *Sansevieria* leaf. Xau now carefully spreads the poison just above the arrowhead – if it were to enter even a tiny scratch on his finger he would cut if off, or die. Some Bushmen, however, prefer to squeeze the poison from the grub directly onto the shaft (88).

81   82
83
84

85 86
87 88

89. To the Bushman the only 'real' way to hunt is with a bow and arrow and a boy does not become a man until he has done so. Sharpened with a file, arrowheads are made from beaten wire.

90, 91. Old Demi annoints himself with a black compound he keeps in an oryx horn to ensure good luck on the hunt, while Bo (91) encourages good fortune by allowing a chameleon to walk across his bow. Like most Bushmen he regards the chameleon with distrust but respects its keen eyesight and deadly hunting prowess.

92. Bo and Taishé tracked this kudu for three arduous days before the poison finally took effect and they could close in for the kill. The entire band came to help carry home the carcase and within a few days every morsel had been eaten.

93. A magnificent bull kudu.

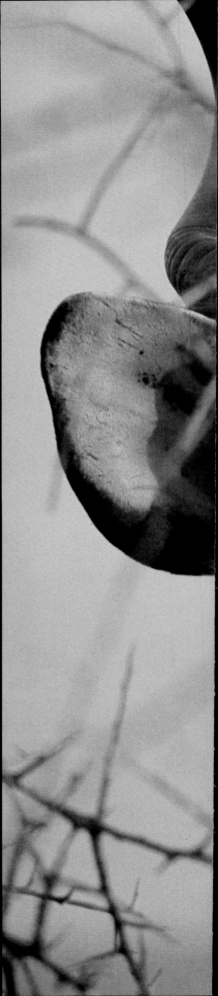

89 90

91 92

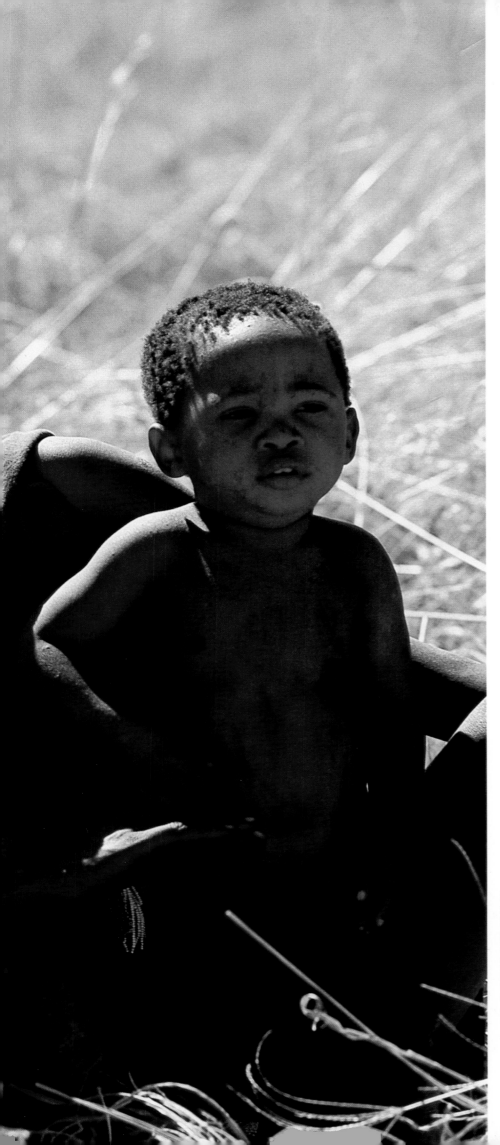

94. Bau grooms her sister's hair while little Toma stands self-contained and completely secure against his mother's body. From birth he knows who he is, his place in the greater order of things and that he need never be alone. If his world remains unchanged he will never have many possessions, yet he will be imbued with something of infinite value – an unshakeable sense of belonging.
95. Amongst the Bushman there is always time for children; to play, to hold, to touch and listen. Here Gao imitates an ostrich trying to escape from the circle of their arms.
96. Humour and experience, intelligence and sensitivity earned through years of hardship and joy have left their imprint on Kushay's face.

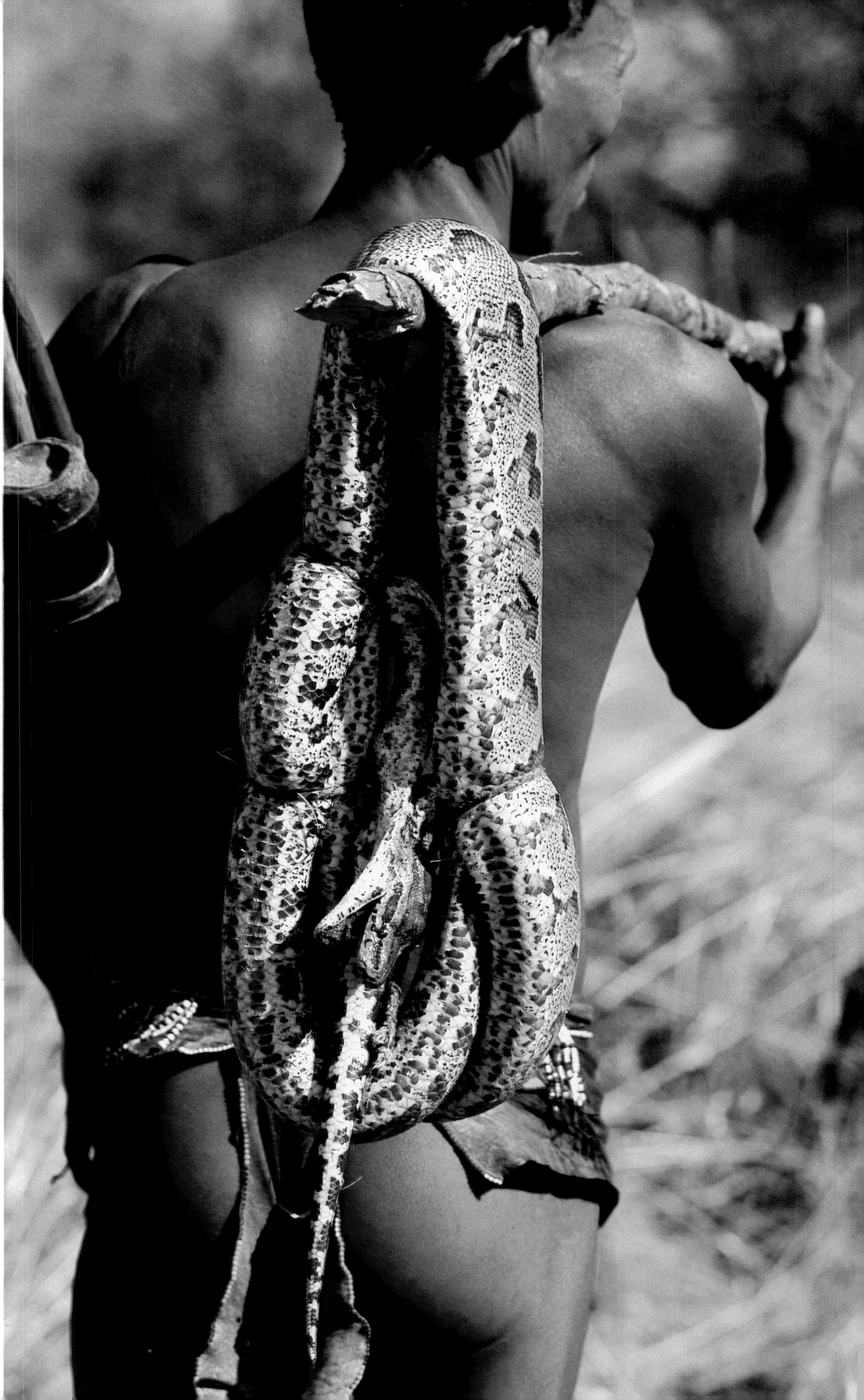

97-101. Bo brings back a three-metre python he caught in a marula tree (97). Dam inspects it intently – adding to his already extraordinary knowledge of his desert environment (98). The boys watch as their father guts the snake. There is no formal teaching among the Bushmen; the children learn simply by observation (99). The prepared python is placed in a hollow lined with hot coals (100) and three hours later it is ready. The meat is rubbery and tastes of fish (101).

102. Firewood piled high as night falls in an area where a pride of lion is hunting. The Bushmen have burned off the undergrowth so that danger cannot approach unseen.

103 104

103. Gaishay, a patriarch of the band, lights his pipe with a stick from the fire. He is one of the few who can remember back to the time when no white man had been seen in his land.

104. Dancing is integral to the Bushman's existence. He dances when he is happy, and he dances to express anxiety and to relieve tension. In accompaniment the glorious voices of the women thrust aside the darkness as they sing, each entering at a different pitch to weave complex and compelling harmonies.

108

105-110. Bees have nested in this gigantic baobab for generations. This band alone has the right to gather honey here as their ancestors did. Taishé watches as Bo first uses a ladder to scale the trunk (105) and then hammers wooden pegs into the soft bark which is scarred by countless holes from previous raids (106). Perched more than ten metres above the ground he subdues the bees with an aromatic smoke and then gently reaches deep into the nest to remove the glistening combs (107). His reward: a precious sweetness which provides much-needed calories in the hard winter months (108). Grimacing with pleasure, Kanha savours the bee grubs – a delicacy reserved for the old people (109) – while Kunta enjoys a rare treat (110).

111. Bo and his children in the temporary camp they had made near a waterhole.

112. A tender moment between grandmother and child.

113. Her husband had given her this kaross as a wedding gift and within its folds she will carry her babies and the food she gathers in the veld. This oryx-hide kaross will last her a lifetime and she has spent many hours of her leisure and imagination decorating it. Another much-prized item of adornment is her necklace of beads; traditionally each one is delicately chipped from the brittle shell of an ostrich egg. The tiny discs are strung onto sinews, then ground to an even size along a special grooved stone and finally given a high polish by being rubbed persistently against the skin.

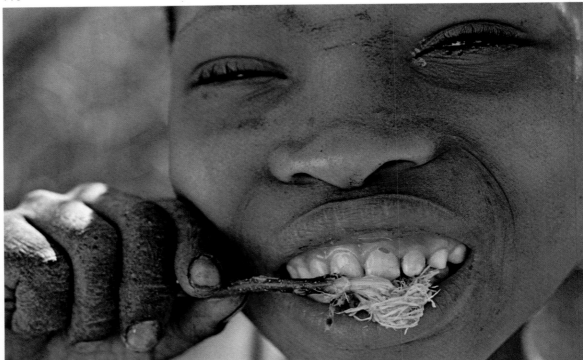

114,115. Bau washes the face of a reluctant Dam; half a mug is more than adequate for a pint-sized baby Bushman.
116. An acacia twig is Dikay's toothbrush. It tastes astringent and leaves his teeth white and shining. Bushmen rarely suffer tooth decay but as they grow older their teeth are ground down by the roughness of their diet.
117. Little Toma's bottom gets a wipe with a handful of dry grass.
118. Qui drinks the bitter liquid from the spongy root of a *Raphionacme burkei*. When water is scarce the Bushman depend on the moisture hidden in tubers and melons.
119. Baobabs loom as monster landmarks against a moonlit Kalahari sky.

ETOSHA: THE PLACE OF DRY WATER

'Etosha' has many meanings but one Owambo described it best of all. He called it 'the place of dry water', his imagery evoking the frequent mirages that dance above the Pan. Imagine a vast inland sea of clay, a bowl-like depression some 6 000 square kilometres in extent set in a National Park the size of Switzerland. Even in the context of Namibia, the scale of the Pan and the park is overwhelming.

For most of the year sun dazzles off the salt-encrusted pan. In winter at sunrise, if you stare out across the aching flatness, it is like watching the sun appear over the earth at the beginning of time. Slowly the great orb rises, flattened, or so it seems by the dust cast up by the winds, and tinted a primordial red by the dust-refracted rays. About it all hangs a brooding silence so intense that it fills the ears with a vacuum of sound. Another day in the millennia of Etosha has begun. Under the winter blaze no clouds form and as the sun climbs higher, dust devils whip across the barren plain. At the day's end the sun lingers, the last rays shooting up like some great veld fire burning just below the evening star.

The Pan may dwindle to a parched wasteland but Etosha National Park is always alive and never more so than when the rains come. Then the Pan is briefly filled and as if from nowhere, overnight, flamingoes in their thousands settle on its surface while all around the great seasonal migrations of game move across the landscape, their movements dictated partly by instinct and partly by the need to claim the best resources.

Thousands of zebra and wildebeest grow sleek on the greening of the earth, while at nearby waterholes, jaws and paws are fastidiously licked clean by feline tongues, before a heavy-bellied sleep.

The Herero, the Owambo, the Thirstland Trekkers – even the Bushman – once hunted here and they have left many names. On the southern boundary of the Etosha National Park there is a low range of hills which the Herero call 'Ondundozonanandana' – 'the place where the young calves used to go and never return'. It is their way of saying that these hills are the haunt of the leopard which loves to feed on the young. In the prosaic manner of our technical age these have now been labelled the Leopard Hills, but the old and beautiful name persists.

The names of the three tourist camps also tell their stories. Namutoni came from the Owambo for the high place which can be seen from afar – although the boggy spring is only slightly higher than the dead-level plain where the historic fort, now a tourist camp, stands. The name of the second camp 'Halali' echoes the traditional hunting horn sounded by the Germans when a stag is brought to bay and the hunt is over. At Etosha, it takes a broader significance for it proclaims that the hunt is indeed over and there will be no further senseless killing within these boundaries. 'Okaukuejo' means in Herero the place of the women, whilst in the far west of the reserve, as yet inaccessible to visitors, lies the place of the young men, 'Otjovasandu'.

Those who know Etosha in all its seasons are constantly aware of the finely-tuned natural balance which exists – complex, fragile, infinitely miraculous. When summer's violent squalls transform the dead world of the Pan it becomes an immense ephemeral lagoon. The shallow tepid water, bitter with dissolved salts and brilliant with sunlight, takes on the colour of turgid pea soup.

Then the flamingoes arrive from distant feeding grounds to dip upturned beaks into the blue-green algae. They need no more than the stars to guide

them, and perhaps the subtle hints of changing daylight lengths and far-off lightning flashes to trigger the deep-seated instinct to migrate.

These pink plumed birds are fastidious breeders. Only if sufficient rain has fallen will they lay their single eggs on the cone-shaped mud nests on the flats. So acutely is their breeding cycle synchronised to the rains and water-level in the Pan that often they go no further than nest building, aborting that season's breeding for a more propitious time. And even in successful years the parents and their fledgling chicks evacuate the Pan only days before it dries to a deathly world of cracked clay.

The flamingo breeding season at Etosha is brief but fascinating. Within a week of hatching the thousands of downy charcoal chicks cluster together, protected from ground predators by the daunting vista of the mud flats. All look alike, all smell alike yet on sound alone the parent finds its own young among the clamouring chicks. Each has an infinitesimal variation of voice which, like the human fingerprint, is uniquely its own. Even before hatching, the parent and chick begin calling to one another in a process known as voice imprintation. What triggers the process is not clearly understood but the result is obvious for by the time the egg hatches there is demonstrable voice recognition which seals the bond between adult and dependent chick. Soon the rapidly developing flamingo young scramble from their mud nests and mass together in nurseries numbering many thousands. Any doubt as to the effectiveness of voice imprintation as a means of recognition between adult and offspring is quelled: the parents leave the thickly packed moving carpets of downy young to look for food and on their return not only find but feed their particular chick. Scientists believe that it is the chick which identifies the parental call, detaching itself from the throng and calling in response. Its reward is a regurgitated soup of semi-digested algae.

But for the flamingo chicks the saga of survival has just begun. Day by day the Pan dries up, leaving the flightless young increasingly isolated from the life-giving waters by stretches of dry mud. Under the blazing Etosha sun the chicks now set off in their race against time. But as they walk towards the drying lagoon so its water recedes ever further. On thin stilt-like legs the young struggle 80 kilometres or more in their trek and all the while the parents relay food and water. Many do not survive this arduous endurance test but those that do, earn their place among the departing flocks as the flamingoes abandon the drying Pan.

Beyond the Pan there is a larger natural world of hoof and horn and fang and claw, the park itself which contains some

50 000 large wild animals and uncountable small mammals, birds and reptiles. The area they roam is so immense and so harsh that it is difficult to conceive the damage done by the few inroads of 'progress'. But every time man erects a fence or puts a bulldozer's blade to the earth, he threatens Nature's master plan. Take something as seemingly innocuous as a tourist road through the veld.

At Etosha it is not adequate to bulldoze a route between game-viewing areas. The talcum powder dust curls from the clay, choking visitors and making it necessary to cover the scraped earth with a substantial layer of limestone gravel. The answer is exquisitely simple yet virulently abusive. Gravel beds lie strewn in abundance – in places only a few centimetres below the Park's surface of sand and clay – but the landscape is so unrelievedly flat that any removal of gravel leaves behind a naked, shallow depression of infertile limey soil in which run-off water accumulates after rain.

'Aha! You see!' the voices of progress proclaim. 'Our work has even provided additional drinking-places for the animals, and right next to the tourist road at that!'

Beware the backlash of injured Nature! So subtly does she react to this scar that her retribution is difficult to foresee and even more difficult to detect. A bacterium invades these man-made pools and flourishes in the alkaline waters. Known to science as *Bacillus anthracis* – or more commonly as anthrax – the bacteria can kill a man or beast if it enters the body. It takes no more than a scratch on the skin or a mild abrasion in the mouth to introduce the deadly bacillus into the blood stream. There it begins to multiply, excreting toxins so virulent that within hours the host suffers an ugly death. Worse is to follow. The cadaver becomes a bloated repository for billions of anthrax bacteria.

Take a single zebra that dies after drinking from one of these infected pools. Vulture and jackal, hyaena and crow snatch and gobble at the remains, scattering anthrax across the veld. Blood from the victim does not coagulate – a characteristic of anthrax – and when it is spilled onto the ground by eager beaks and snapping teeth, it exposes the bacteria to oxygen which signals the single-celled organism to clothe itself in a protective capsule to withstand dessication and the cleansing rays of the sun. In this sporulated form anthrax can remain viable for a decade or more, retaining its ability to deal death to the drinker of water or eater of grass onto which it adheres.

Strangely enough, the flesh-eating scavengers, including the lion, seem quite tolerant of the disease. But they act as mechanical carriers of the bacterial spores, infecting waterholes far and near when they leave the carcase to slake

121

their thirst. The vulture is particularly effective at spreading anthrax. It habitually engorges itself and then, to make space for water, regurgitates part of its meal, sometimes into the very water that other thirsty zebra, wildebeest or springbuck will drink.

Such is the deadly process set into motion by the artificial gravel pit. Even the dust around the long-dead zebra is fraught with danger. Inhaled with dust particles, the encapsulated anthrax can rapidly enter the membranes of the lungs to continue its death-evoking cycle.

The gravelled road ensures the visitor a reasonably comfortable ride, but there is an exacting price to pay.

The men who record, calculate and evaluate Nature's bounty – and man's meddling – at Etosha are dedicated ecologists: the zoologist, the botanist, the ornithologist and veterinarian all have a place here, and their tools are many and varied. From the perspex bubble of a helicopter a scientist drones into his tape recorder: 'Zebra, five and one foal, zebra . . . kudu, two bulls, seven cows and three calves, kudu . . .' always naming the animal species before and after the number counted to avoid misinterpretation when the tape is later transcribed. So it is possible to state, with some measure of confidence, that in 1978 there were at least 26 000 springbuck, 10 000 zebra, 2 500 wildebeest and 1 200 elephant in the Etosha National Park. But not all species can be counted in this way. Lion, for instance, are only flushed from cover when the down-wash of the powerful blades and the throatiness of the engine passes directly over them. Other species, too, such as hyaena and rhino are best counted from the ground at watering-places at full moon.

Once ecologists have ascertained how the game population is structured their next task is to determine the migration habits and condition of certain 'target' species. It would be premature to study the lion who sits atop the food pyramid without first knowing something of the prey he hunts. So the veterinarian trains his dart gun at the major herbivores such as the zebra, wildebeest and oryx.

It is an ordeal for darter and darted. Only complete dedication will induce a man to sit harnessed into a tiny seat bolted onto the front of a stripped-down truck which is specially modified and over-powered to enable a high-speed chase over rocks and antbear holes. Flying grit strikes his goggles as truck and wildebeest career across the veld, lurching wildly from side to side, until finally the dart syringe injects its load of morphine derivatives into vital muscle and the pursuer can slacken off, waiting for the tell-tale symptoms: unevenness of gait, hunching of the hind quarters and blind goose-stepping. In less than five minutes the wildebeest is down. The sweaty thrill of the chase is replaced by the clinical probing of stethoscope and syringe. The heartbeat is monitored and small quantities of blood drawn off to be analysed with precision to indicate the animal's physiological condition. Even a dental impression is made to assess age. The final indignity is the fitting of a brightly coloured and boldly numbered neckband that will stay with the animal until it dies.

An antidote is injected into an ear vein and within minutes the wildebeest is on its feet, plunging away across the veld. From now on, dawn to dusk observations will show frequency of resting, grazing and drinking as well as social encounters such as fighting or mating among recognised animals. Days and months of patient watching and recording under a burning Etosha sun and cool moon will become data electronically computed, the results flowing out faster than the mind can comprehend.

Seasonally the animal herds of Etosha migrate back and forth in an arc around the Pan which serves as a fulcrum for this great pendulum of movement. In the fulness of summer, moisture gathers on the eastern horizon, billowing into massive thunderheads which move across the bleached plains. Depending on the whim of the wind either rain or drought can triumph. In good years the rain's force is torrential as cumulonimbus clouds mount over Etosha. Then grass seeds germinate in the once sun-baked ground and within days the earth is mantled in the most exuberant of greens.

But before the rain falls, the zebra and wildebeest are already alert to its coming. They become restless in their winter grazing grounds and family groups merge into herds for the long trek from Andoni plains to the east of the Park, around the southern fringes of Etosha Pan to the lure of Okaukuejo's sweet grasses which will soon sprout 150 kilometres further west. Within a day or so Andoni lies deserted and the spectacle of one of the last remaining

121. For thousands of years this great Pan was the focus of all the waterways of northern Namibia and gradually an immense bed of silt and clay accumulated. Even the great Kunene once emptied here before geological upheaval directed its course to the sea. Today the Pan seldom floods extensively and herds of zebra and wildebeest tread its intricate tracery of game trails to graze its islands of grass.
122. Nostrils flare as a springbuck chases a rival.
123. During the winter months increasing numbers of elephant have begun to visit Etosha's permanent waterholes.

migrations in Africa is under way: tens of thousands of animals are on the move. Long lines of zebra plod across the dusty plains, drawn unerringly to the distant thunderstorms. Pausing only to snatch at last season's tufts of grass along the way, the herds move on, skirting thicket and tree-clump and drinking briefly at unaccustomed waterholes. It is a dangerous time for mares heavy with foals for they are the obvious victims in encounters with lion during the trek across unfamiliar veld.

In contrast to the stoically plodding zebras, the wildebeest travel in bursts of comical frenzy, their horns scything and hooves stamping at imagined dangers. Sometimes the wildebeest lag behind the zebra, at other times they are out in front, prancing and tossing their heads.

For the Andoni lions who remain behind, the exodus brings with it the spectre of starvation. Bound by their hunting territories they cannot follow the migrating herds and must now lower themselves to lesser prey. Not even the guinea fowl or raucous korhaan will escape the lions' attention in these empty days. But as the Andoni prides become gaunt, so Okaukeujo's lion population sleeks, the hunger pangs of the past winter unremembered as they launch out on a summer evening's hunt, the scent of zebra delicious on the evening breeze.

The great cats are inherently lazy during the day's heat, languid in the scant shade of the trees. One researcher who studied their metabolism likened them to giant batteries of muscle which expend almost all their power during the stalk and the short sprint to the kill.

Towards evening, when muscles have been toned and flexed after the day's rest, lion and lioness muster their terrible strength for the hunt. And this is never more memorable than when lion and thunderstorm dominate the veld. The combination of thunder and violent lightning seems to confuse the game herds, while the winds play havoc with scent and hearing. Lions, always the opportunist killers, exploit this confusion and hunt mercilessly among the disorientated herds. Few sights at Etosha are more impressive than a pride of lions moving out in hunting formation under an impending storm. This is the lion in his element – a deadly efficient killing machine. After these wild, storm-inspired hunts the morning sun reveals carcases strewn across the plain, many of them uneaten victims of an orgy of blood lust.

Rain is the signal for the elephant herds to move north, seeking to drink and bathe in the fresh rainwater collected in small pans. These giants, 'the grey ghosts of the bush', move soundlessly on cushioned feet, following ancient paths which lead to the best pools and choicest food, often outside the sanctuary of the park. Along the way they may pause to rub against the dead stumps of the Omumborombonga trees which become polished by pachydermal skin over the decades. Local tribal lore has it that this is the tree of life from which the first animals and humans arose. They call it 'the ancestor tree' and leave it alone out of respect for the spirits it once harboured.

There is no autumn or spring in this world, only the short, intense rainy season, from January to April, followed by winter's brief dry chill and the angry heat that precedes the summer rains. As the transitory grasses of summer wither, the living pendulum of migrating animals begins to swing back across the veld. Now Andoni's winter grassland will be their home until the rain returns. And so, the green flush of summer advances and recedes over Etosha National Park, taking with it the living and leaving behind the dead.

124. After the kill a cheetah and her cub keep an uneasy eye on the mother kudu as she circles her dead foal.
125. A lion and lioness sleek in the sun.
126. Resplendent in the colours of the old German Empire, the crimson-breasted shrike is popularly called the 'Reichsvogel'.
127. A cluster of giraffe at Etosha.

128-131. Rampant zebra stallions battle for dominance at a waterhole. The air is punctuated by their fierce yapping and barking as they lunge at neck and fetlock in their struggle for control of the mares and possession of territory.

132. Still too young to be affected by rivalry, a zebra foal looks on. No two zebra have the same pattern of stripes and scientists in the field easily recognise individuals.

133. Elephant coat themselves with the talcum powder of the Pan – a fine limestone dust which cools and insulates.

134. According to !Kung Bushman lore there was a magical time when the animal and the human world were one. It was a time when the trickster God reigned and he had as his servant the kori bustard. And when this era came to an end it was, so the Bushman believe, the kori bustard that made one animal different from the next. He built a fire and in it placed the irons with which he gave the zebra its stripes, the giraffe its patterns, the leopard its spots, and all creatures their distinctive markings. The Bushman say: 'Before this we were all people together, but after this we were divided each to his own.' Perhaps it was this former grandeur that gives this bird its haughty strut.
135. A yellow-billed hornbill – cocky denizen of the bush birdworld.
136. A symmetry of springbuck drinking at one of Etosha's several springs.
137. Gregarious creatures of Namibia's arid land, ground squirrels assume a typical erect stance.

134 135 137
136

138. A wide variety of birds are associated with the tenement-like nests of the social weaver: some are simply uninvited guests that shelter here and others, such as the pygmy falcon use it as a breeding-place. But for the social weaver, the most dreaded predators of all are snakes which enter the nest and slither from chamber to chamber eating eggs and young.

139. A panoply of blue cranes, zebra and wildebeest in serried ranks at the edge of one of Etosha's many waterholes.

140. Grounded in the early cool, a pair of white-backed vultures wait patiently for the air to heat up. Only then do they lift their ungainly bodies into the sky using the thermal air currents that rise off the Pan, soaring so high that they appear mere specks. From this lofty vantage-point the birds disperse, scanning for carcases and at the same time keeping an eye on one another. No sooner does one begin to descend than the others, as if at a signal, converge on the spot. In this way the vultures are able to search collectively over a far wider area than if functioning alone.

141. The oryx is remarkable for its ability to withstand the rigours of the desert. Unable to escape the heat, its body temperature rises so high that its blood would destroy the animal's brain cells. In a unique adaptation, blood destined for the brain is first cooled by circulating through a network of capillaries in the oryx's nasal passages.

142. Zebra stand unperturbed as dust swirls over Etosha's wastes.

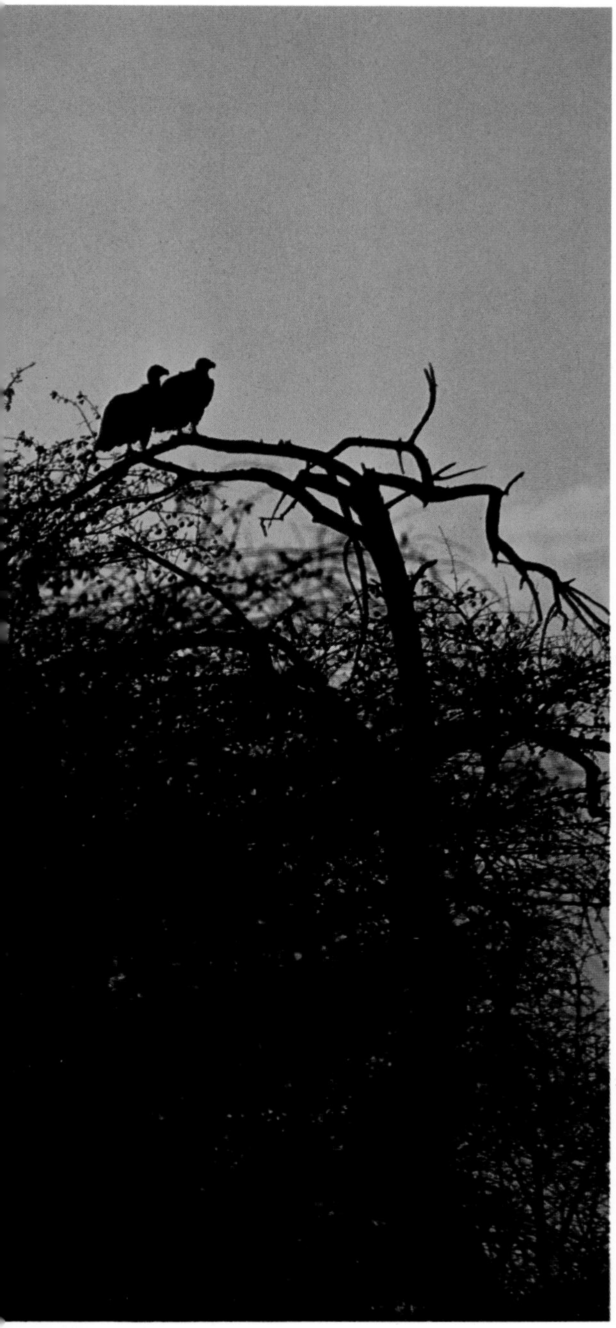

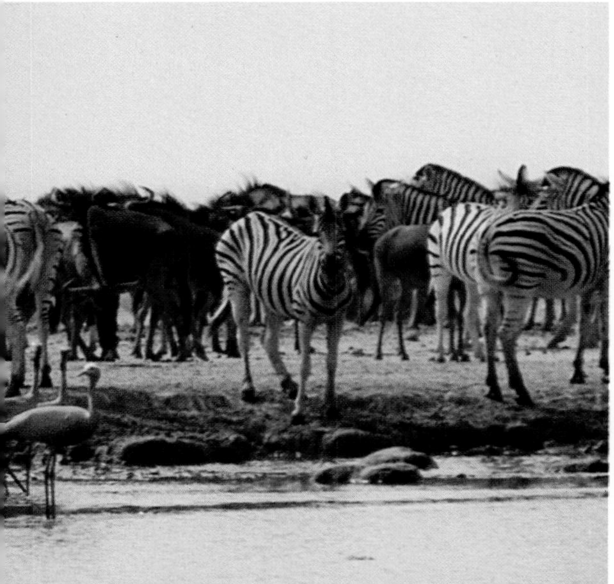

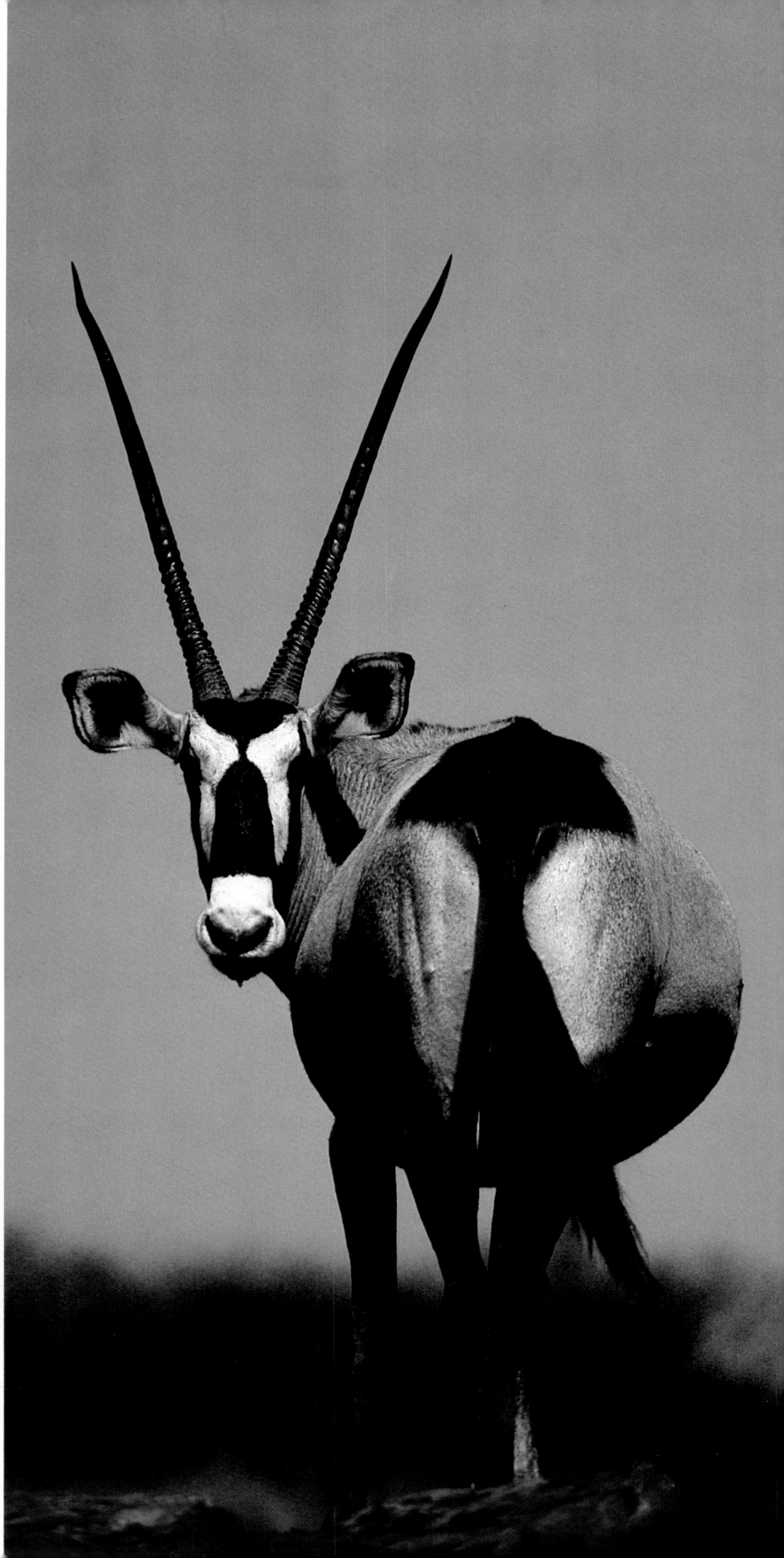

143. The Ekuma River, one of the Pan's major feeders, straggles in from the north.

144. Constantly on the move, great herds of zebra and wildebeest follow long-established trails that criss-cross the Pan and its surrounds.

145. The celebrated gentleman hunter Cornwallis Harris wrote of the wildebeest: 'Of all quadrupeds the gnoo is probably the most awkward and grotesque. Nature doubtless formed him in one of her freaks, and it is scarcely possible to contemplate his ungainly figure without laughter . . . This ever-wary animal has at once a ferocious and ludicrous appearance.'

148

146. A red-necked falcon tugs at a morsel.
147. A startling image that evokes the many-headed Hydra – in reality a harmless yellow-bellied sandsnake beginning to moult.
148. The gentle remains of a rosy-faced lovebird lie discarded on the ground.

149. Incredible though it may seem, as many as 3 000 pairs of pelicans choose the complete isolation of the dry Etosha Pan to lay their clutch of eggs. Here they rear their chicks, protected from predators by the hot white emptiness. But pelicans need fish and fish need water. The nearest fishing ground to this breeding colony is Lake Oponono (a part of which is shown on the following page), 100 kilometres to the north-west. But to fly there and back would consume so much energy that the effort would nullify any gain. So the pelicans, masters of gliding, catch the lifting air thermals that rise from the shimmering Pan. Only a few, economical wing-beats and they soar upward. Soon the air is filled with great white bodies, turning and turning in a sky-bound vortex towards Oponono. Each parent makes the journey alternately, returning the following day, their stomachs filled. As they commence their descent to the nests, their webbed feet act as air-brakes and the wind rushes through their extended pinions. With a minimum of effort the Etosha pelicans airlift 1 000 tonnes of fish to their nests during the four-month breeding period: a round trip of 200 kilometres each alternate day.
150. As the new season's waters spread over the Pan, flamingoes in their thousands converge on Etosha.

THE PEOPLE OF THE EFUNDJA

When only four days old the Owambo infant is taken to the homestead entrance and shown its world: the well tilled plains, the muddy-banked oshanas and the fruit-laden trees of Owamboland. At the same time it is introduced symbolically to its future rôle: a boy is shown the milk containers and the cattle; a girl, the threshing floor and great squat granary baskets.

In the traditional way of life of the Owambo there is no ambiguity as to status and the distinctions are clearly drawn between the sexes. As soon as a boy can handle a bow and arrow and throw his club, he cares for the smallstock near the homestead. In his teens he is sent to collect salt at the salt pans and is entrusted with the herds at the cattle-post some distance from his home. From the men in his life – his father, his maternal uncle, his siblings – he learns of his adult responsibilities towards the cattle which give him status and his family milk and butter; he learns how to care for the elaborately palisaded homestead in which his wife and children will live; he learns the pleasures of the hunt, his duties at council meetings and, in the past, his commitment to war.

According to the traditional division of labour men work with the animals, women work in the fields and care for the household. There is some overlap in that it is a man's duty to build the family homestead and do the hard physical work of breaking in new land. Cutting and transporting the thick mopane poles for the walls of the huts and palisade of a new homestead is no small undertaking and even today with the help of saws, axes and light trucks it is a major task.

From the air the labyrinthine homesteads create bold patterns. The passages which at ground level twist and turn without apparent reason, from above form a well-integrated whole, hut linked to hut and courtyard to courtyard.

A chief or headman's kraal and homestead are imposing, the encircling palisade some 200 metres in diameter and 2,5 to 3 metres high. An ordinary homestead is about 20 to 30 metres across and contains separate huts for the husband, his wife – formerly his wives for the Owambo were polygamous until Christianity entrenched monogamy – the young men, girls and visitors. The huts are for sleeping; during the day people sit in the courtyards beneath open-sided shelters with thatched roofs.

In the past when the Owambo waged war with neighbouring peoples and raided cattle from one another these structures made superb defensive positions. Hidden behind a stout palisade, a single man stabbing through the crevices could keep an army at bay.

During a visit to Owamboland in 1867, the explorer Charles Andersson wondered at these distinctive edifices and remarked that nothing less than a cannon would make any impression on them. But apart from its traditional defensive rôle, the homestead with its encircling thornbrush kraal also offers sanctuary for the cattle and protection for the granary baskets perched high on their stilt-like legs, the wooden milk containers and the sunken mortars in which the women pound grain into meal.

Some time in the 16th century when the Owambo first came to settle in what is now the north-eastern part of Namibia, the immense plain was covered with fine woodland interlaced with oshanas, the watercourses that drain the annual flood, efundja, from Angola. But generation after generation of Owambo felled the trees to make new homesteads and to clear the land for tilling so that now only the wild fruit trees protected by taboo remain.

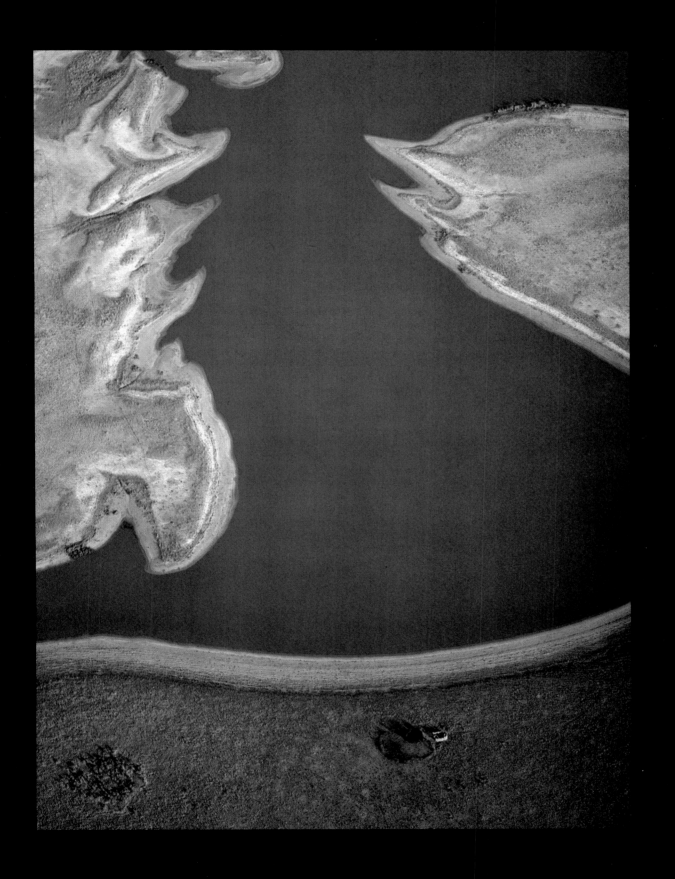

Most useful of all is the palm (Hyphaene ventricosa). Its abundant fruits are eaten and brewed into a popular drink, its fronds are plaited into baskets and mats, the ribs make excellent bows – and a feared instrument of chastisement – while the sap is tapped and brewed into a highly intoxicating liquor.

Now that so much of the land is cleared the beautiful wild fruit trees stand alone in the fields amid the bald monotony of the Owamboland landscape. But also conspicuous in the landscape are the figures of women going about their ever-recurring tasks in the home and in the fields. Their efforts are well-rewarded for the land is fertile and the annual flooding of the plain brings life-giving silt to feed the crops of the new season. Occasionally, when the flood fails to come down, the Owambo suffer great hardship for not only is there insufficient rainfall in many parts of Owamboland to sustain the herds and crops, but the vast quantities of bream and pink-bellied barbel carried by the efundja are a major item in the Owambo diet. Trapped in nets and fishing baskets, the fish are eaten fresh or smoked and dried to be eaten later as a relish with porridge or even traded.

In the fields grow millet, sorghum, beans, pumpkin, sweet potato and groundnuts while, according to the season, the wild trees provide a nutritious crop of fleshy marula, ebony berries, sweet wild figs and bird plum, protein-rich manketti nuts and the tart-flavoured fruit of the baobab tree. In common with most other Bantu-speaking people the Owambo only slaughter cattle on ceremonial occasions, but they regularly eat goat, chicken and dog.

Among the Owambo descent is matrilineal. Hence a person belongs to the clan and lineage of his mother, although paternity in fact or law is acknowledged. Children, however, take their mother's clan name and traditionally their maternal uncle has more authority over them than their natural father. Because they inherit from him and not from their father it follows that this uncle has first claim on them, and from him the children will eventually inherit the fruits of their own labour.

The complexity of the matrilineal system is well illustrated in the rules governing the choice of a marriage partner. The children of two sisters have the same clan name and are therefore considered to belong to the same family and cannot marry. But the children of a brother and sister in a matrilineal society have different clan names and although they too are first cousins they are regarded as belonging to different families and are considered ideal marriage partners.

At first glance the system appears to work well: by tradition a man's estate goes to his sister's children and his own inherit from their maternal uncle. But within this system lie inherent conflicts not readily apparent. Traditional Owambo society gives the impression that everyone lives an unhurried existence, tied to the seasons, but otherwise unchanging. In the eyes of outsiders it appears to be a life perhaps limited in self-expression and individual achievement yet rich in peace of mind. But the system is changing: it has been for a long time. Some claim that the breakdown of the traditional way of life is a direct result of the intrusion of western civilization; more accurately this has been an accelerating factor, not a causative one.

When Francis Galton – natural scientist, explorer and first white man to penetrate the desert and thornveld shielding Owamboland – reached this broad plain in 1853 the people he found living among the oshanas of the north were strong and well-established. There was honey and porridge and the cattle were sleek and fat. In the four centuries since the Owambo had crossed the Okavango swamps in the north and settled here they had prospered and grown numerous. Yet the society that Galton saw was in fact one already in the grip of radical change.

As part of the great southward migration of Bantu-speaking people, the Owambo had been predominantly agricultural and the mother, as tiller of the soil, maintained her position as central figure in the matrilineal system. In this new homeland blessed with the efundja the Owambo had seen their herds and flocks increase at a prodigious rate and with prosperity came changing attitudes. The male became more dominant in Owambo society and his desire to have a say in things rose in direct proportion to his contribution to the family wealth and status. His own children took cattle from him and on Owamboland's rich pastures their herds increased; in the process they became more independent. There was no longer as great a compulsion to go and live in an uncle's homestead to inherit his herds; a young man could now draw wealth and status directly from his own father.

When a man died his children tried to retain as many of his cattle as they could while the nephews, in terms of their matrilineal rights, tried to claim as many as possible from their grasping cousins. When this happened in the clan of a chief, the heir to the chieftainship suddenly found that one of the sources of his position – namely the wealth in cattle that enabled him to care for his subjects in time of need – was being usurped and his power was declining.

With the shaking off of the bonds of economic dependence on one's mother's family came other pressures. Intercession with the ancestral spirits lay with one's maternal uncle and in renouncing the matrilineal system a man also jeopardised this basic aspect of traditional belief. At this point, in the late 1800s, Christianity and western civilization reached Owamboland and quickly filled the gaps of a social structure loosening at its joints.

The missionaries entering Owamboland offered a new religion that stressed the individual and provided an alternative means of spiritual fulfilment, one divorced from intrafamily obligations and conflicts. The immediate result was that the Owambo in overwhelming numbers embraced Christianity.

Change that had begun long before with the prosperity achieved by the Owambo in their new homeland, now moved ahead at a faster pace. Traders brought new economic concepts dominated by the profit motive. Education and training offered an alternative method of achieving status. A new class emerged, educated in western ways and freed by the security of a cash income from the bonds of reciprocity and traditional family obligations.

Today the original seven tribes that followed the silvery waters of the oshanas make up a large and forceful sector, 46 per cent of the total Namibian population. Many Owambo have become contract workers on the mines and industries elsewhere in the country, some have left their traditional homes to settle in distant towns, but the majority maintain their identity as the people of the efundja.

152. Less than a century ago the pioneer explorer Charles Andersson wrote of Owamboland: 'It is a beautiful, open, and for Africa highly cultivated country, environed on all sides with interminable and dense forests – in short a perfect oasis in the desert.' Yet as one looks across this same vista today the only trees that remain are those protected by taboo. Here ploughed fields await the efundja (flood) which will bestow fertility over the land. But in years when the flood fails to come down the reality of over-exploitation becomes apparent: then Owamboland is closer to desert than the 'oasis' at which Andersson marvelled.

153 154 155

153. An Owambo homestead – a complex maze of hidden chambers, dead-ends and narrow passages designed to baffle would-be intruders.
154. Cattle gather to drink along one of the two major canals that lead water from the Kunene River to slake Owamboland's thirst. The Hyphaene palms that stud much of this region are a rich source of food, drink and weaving material.
155. These young girls already know what their traditional adult rôles will be: Here they carry freshly winnowed and ground corn to the kitchen area.

156. The war in Angola has brought many refugees into Owamboland, among whom are skilled woodcarvers, and this design, worked in kiaat, is typical of Kavango craftsmanship.

157. Nimble fingers weave a basket from vegetable-dyed strips from Hyphaene palm fronds.

158. Owamboland is renowned for its skilled basket-makers whose wares are much in demand both locally and for the tourist trade.

159. In her underground pottery an Owambo housewife rubs down her pots before firing them in a pit fueled by burning cattle dung. She had excavated her workshop beneath a termite heap so that humidity would be relatively high and stable and in these conditions her pots can dry slowly and evenly.

156 157
158 159

160. An old Owambo man in woven hat.

161. In the far north a Kavango livestock inspector pedals from kraal to kraal checking for diseased cattle. Wherever he goes he carries his bow and arrow in case he should come across a guineafowl or steenbuck to bag for the family cooking pot.

162. While mother works in the fields, the new baby is entrusted to his elder sister's care.

163. End-of-year exams for a pupil at the Linus Shashipapo school on the banks of the Okavango.

164. As the first rainstorm of the season approaches, a herder sets fire to the undergrowth along a stretch of the Okavango River. The rains will soon turn the charred earth green and his cattle will grow fat on the new shoots.

165. Darkness falls on a homestead over which kiaat trees tower.
166. Hippo are the undisputed masters of the Okavango River. When they show their molars and bellow, the canoes go scurrying to the banks – nothing can induce the villagers to challenge this authority.

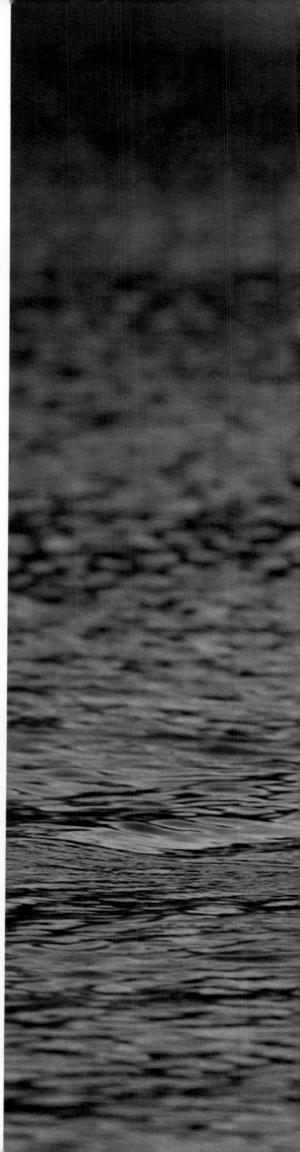

165 166

167

168

167. In threatening pose, a looper caterpillar reacts to danger.
168. A shimmer of butterflies sip from the damp mud of an *omuramba* (watercourse).
169. On a leaf filigreed by a feeding tortoise beetle, an egg case glistens.
170. After the rains, blood lilies in their thousands push through the wet earth and ornament the Okavango River banks.
171. Taxi of the Okavango, dug-out canoes such as this one ferry the river people and their possessions to and fro.

THE PEOPLE OF KAOKO~ LAND

In the far north of Namibia where the Kunene River marks the border with Angola, the sound of stone on wood could still be heard 50 years ago. Venture deep into a copse of mopane, and you might still find a man, his skin gleaming with pigmented fat, willing to demonstrate how to fell a tree with a stone adze. For a moment it seems as if time is in reverse; but the impression is as misleading as the image is fleeting, for change is inexorable and the Stone Age in Kaokoland is long since past.

Yet few societies in the world have resisted new ideas to the extent of the Herero-speaking Himba and their neighbours in Kaokoland. Their natural conservatism, coupled with the geographic isolation of their 50 000 square kilometre territory and its inhospitable terrain, have left them largely untouched by the ravages and rewards of western civilization.

They are locked from the sea by the desolate Skeleton Coast with its bleak white beaches which give way, as one moves away from the shore, to barren gravel flats and salt-encrusted pans.

Inland lies the Kaokoveld, a remote region of dry broken hills and rugged mountain ranges that merge in the east with the featureless sands of the northern Kalahari. Kaokoland is naturally inaccessible and an almost impenetrable barrier of 'red tape' has until recently made this region *terra incognita* to all but a handful of outsiders. The fortunate few who visited Kaokoland returned with tantalizing accounts of its magnificent scenery, its wildlife and its fascinating peoples. Inevitably many of these accounts were romanticised and exaggerated but reality does not lag far behind, for it is indeed a land of dramatic contrasts and austere beauty. The gaunt Baynes and Otjihipa Mountains soar while the Kunene River gorges plunge, the gentle dolomite hills of the south give way to the rugged peaks and broad valleys of the west. Even the seasons are extreme. The formidable heat of spring gives way to the short, fierce rainy season which transforms dusty flats into water-logged vleis, and sandy watercourses into brief but raging torrents.

In this land that knows few intruders we observe, from a lofty promontory in the Pro-Namib, the unfolding of a single day. To the east, silhouetted by the rising sun, the jagged outlines of the escarpment tower in a confusion of twisted strata. Extending from the escarpment are the contrasting flat summits of outlying ranges floating like a fleet of giant ships in the soft morning mist. The layer of basalt that caps many of these mountains is testimony of one of the most spectacular periods in the Earth's history when, in early Jurassic times, the super-continent of Gondwanaland broke up and much of what is now southern Africa was racked by volcanic activity such as the world has never since experienced.

As the sun rises the mist begins to roll back towards the coast, disclosing ranges of much lower relief, often little more than ridges of massive pink and grey granite boulders. Through the ages, countless searing days and frosty nights have blistered and cracked the outer layers of these rocks, littering the surface with shattered fragments.

The last wisps of mist disperse, and in the soft morning light our gaze is drawn out over an immense panorama of broad valleys broken by steep-sided mountains and stark outcrops of exposed rock. Traversing the valleys are meandering dry watercourses which vary in size from small flood channels to wide sandy riverbeds, sometimes more than 100 metres across.

But beneath the dry sands there is often water in considerable quantities although it rarely flows on the surface – except in years of exceptional rain.

The broad plains reaching out from the mountains are sand and gravel, and appear devoid of all vegetation; but on closer examination they reveal a sparse covering of dried and withered tufts of desert grass, one of the wonders of the Pro-Namib. When more than just a scattering of showers fall, they stand tall and lush, transforming the plain into a vast wind-rippled sea of bright emerald. Within weeks the seed-heads ripen to shades of yellow and silvery white that contrast strikingly with the deep green of the younger shoots.

When the desert blooms and water shimmers in the rain-filled pans, Hartmann's mountain zebra wind down the rocky passes from the highlands and join the oryx, springbuck and Burchell's zebra below the escarpment. Then great congregations of wildlife graze hock-deep in the new grasses, but scenes of such magnificent colour are seldom repeated more than once or twice a decade. Within months of the last rains, the scorching sun and winds dry the pans and bleach the grass a uniform pale yellow. And as the dry season progresses, sometimes extending over many years, the herds once more disperse into the mountains in search of the parched but palatable blades of grass that remain on the more inaccessible slopes.

The larger watercourses and riverbeds are marked by dark margins of shrubs and trees, but the plains themselves are largely bare. On the rocky mountain slopes and along the dry rivercourses the most conspicuous plants are the *Commiphoras,* the short spreading trees or shrubs renowned in biblical times for their precious resin, myrrh. On the slopes of the escarpment they are very common, giving way, as the rainfall increases eastward, to the ubiquitous mopane *(Colophospermum mopane)* and the purple-pod terminalia which dominate much of the Kaokoveld highlands, often forming dense woodland.

The sun is now well above the horizon and the deep shadows that eclipsed the west-facing slopes recede. As yet there is no whisper of a breeze. Not a leaf rustles, not an animal stirs. Our eyes sweep across the landscape, searching for the slightest evidence that this is not a lifeless canvas.

Faintly, at first, we hear the soft chirping of a lark. Then other sounds drift up from the valley; the distinctive 'kelkiewyn' calls of Namaqua sandgrouse winging their way to a distant spring, the frog-like croaking of a pair of Rüppel's korhaan, and in the stunted trees along a shallow watercourse, the gentle cooing of laughing doves. A few metres away a large lizard scuttles noisily across the weathered rocks and just below us an unseen jackal gives a last piercing yelp before retiring to its shadowy lair. The new day has begun.

Now that the sun has climbed above the horizon the temperature rises rapidly. Already the plains are beginning to shimmer and within a few hours the heat will rise in waves off the baking sand. Across the valley there is movement; what we had previously taken to be a few low bushes are in fact three oryx grazing the stubble of last summer's grass.

A stone tumbling down a steep slope announces a mountain zebra mare picking her way along a narrow ledge. After a few steps she stops and carefully surveys the ground in front. We freeze in our positions only 50 metres above, but she looks neither above nor behind and continues down the path. Thirty metres behind her a second mare appears on the same tortuous path and soon a third, followed closely by a small foal, comes into view. A large immaculately striped stallion brings up the rear. The lead mare stops, and again her keen eyes search for any sign of danger ahead. As if at a signal the others stop too, but soon all move on down the path. As

we watch, the five zebra cautiously descend to the plain and walk, still in single file but without pausing, to a broad riverbed where they are lost among the tall trees fringing the banks. The lead zebra soon reappears and, after another long careful look about her, starts to dig with her forefeet in the sandy bed. She continues to dig, occasionally checking for danger until, satisfied with her efforts, she lowers her head and drinks from the water that has welled up in the sandy depression. When all the zebra have drunk they leave the riverbed and return to their rocky fastness. Within a few minutes a small group of springbuck, until then unnoticed among the riverine vegetation, cross the sand and drink from the hole dug by the zebra.

Upriver, in a grove of tall acacias, the crown of a camelthorn shakes violently. A few moments later a large bull elephant moves out of the shrubbery and walks towards the base of another camelthorn giving it a short, powerful push that sends 20 or 30 large grey pods raining down. Using its trunk as a sensitive detector, the elephant locates these highly nutritious pods, delicately picks them up and eats them. After a short rest the bull moves on, passing a smallish mopane from which he breaks a young branch. Then, holding the thick end firmly in his trunk, he draws the branch through his mouth in such a way that his great molars tear off the bark and most of the leaves before the stripped wood is discarded.

During the hot dry months preceding the first summer rains, when the dessicating winds have drawn the moisture from all but the most succulent plants, large numbers of elephant congregate along the major riverbeds of the Pro-Namib to exploit the relatively lush vegetation and protein-rich acacia pods. In the rainy season these same herds disperse across the vast trackless ranges and valleys of the escarpment and adjoining mountains where they are seldom seen.

The sun is now past its zenith and has begun its long, slow descent towards the western horizon. The all-pervading heat is only momentarily relieved by the occasional soft, leaf-fluttering breezes. Below us the plains are once more still and apparently lifeless, but unseen beneath the trees and bushes and rocky ledges the creatures of the Kaokoveld rest, patiently waiting for the burning sands to cool sufficiently for them to resume their daily activities.

We gaze out drowsily over the plains only vaguely comprehending the scene before us, and it is some time before we fully register a large cloud of dust rising from the crest of a low saddle that leads into an adjoining valley. As we peer into the billowing dust we discern the gaunt features of more than 100 long-horned mottled cattle moving steadily towards us. Striding out in front are two tall powerfully-built Himba youths dressed only in long skin aprons. Each carries a wooden staff and a broad-bladed throwing spear with the skin and brush of an oryx tail drawn over the shaft. They walk straight to the riverbed – a short distance downstream from where the zebra drank earlier – to a low thorny brush fence which encloses a shallow pit. Within this enclosure is a large hollowed-out trough cut from the heavy trunk of a leadwood tree. The young men promptly start clearing out the sand and deepening the pit and as they dig, clear water oozes from the bottom so that soon there is a fairly deep pool.

The leading cattle reach the river and mill about outside the enclosure, the smell of water strong in their nostrils. Some of them discover the small hole dug by the zebra but in their

173. The remote and beautiful Marienfluss in north-west Kaokoland, where vast areas of delicately coloured desert sands lie entrapped between rugged mountains of bare rock.

frenzy to drink trample it within seconds into a hoof-churned patch of damp earth. Their thirst still unquenched, they collect around the enclosure lowing and shuffling restlessly while the youths finish their work.

Two more Himba arrive, one carrying a bucket roughly carved from the soft white wood of the marula tree. Fat and sweat glisten on his skin as he begins pailing water into the hollow log. The nearest animals are now allowed to drink at the trough, and while one youth maintains the water level the other controls the jostling beasts with his long staff so that only five or six animals drink at a time. While the men patiently water their herd we observe them more closely.

All four wear similar leather aprons and skin sandals, but the most obvious difference in their appearance is their hairstyles. The two older men wear large turbans of softened sheepskin stretched taut over their uncut hair. The heads of the two youths, on the other hand, are smooth shaven but for a strip of hair over the crown of their heads which is plaited into a single shoulder-length pigtail. Only when they marry will they, too, don the turban. Around their necks are various bulky necklaces, and one of the younger men also wears a loose single-strand necklace to which are attached four wedge-shaped pieces of leather, cut from the ears of heifers presented to him by his father at name-giving, initiation and various other ceremonies during his childhood. According to Himba custom only these gift heifers and their progeny are inherited by the son on his father's death. All other livestock and material possessions will belong to his father's younger brother or, if none survives, the eldest son of his father's eldest sister. However, the eldest son will inherit from his father the holy fire sticks that signify his position as spiritual head of the family.

For the Himba man life revolves almost exclusively around the care of his herds. To him there is no other way of measuring wealth or status except in terms of cattle: if a man has many, he is rich, a *muhona;* if he has few, he is poor, a *musyona;* if he has no cattle at all, he is called a *mutjimba,* a man of no status and is looked down upon because he must dig in the ground for his food.

But his livestock are more than just a symbol. Although he may cultivate some maize, pumpkins and gourds wherever the harsh environment permits, it is a man's cattle, goats and fat-tailed sheep that provide food for his family. Cow's milk soured with various curdling agents forms the basis of the Himba diet. They only eat their cattle on ceremonial occasions or when an animal dies, but smallstock are periodically slaughtered for meat. The skins are an important raw material used for making sleeping mats, blankets, carrying bags, various pouches, as well as almost everything the Himba wear.

What they cannot provide for themselves they purchase with their livestock from neighbouring tribes, some of whom have become specialists in various crafts or essential services. Most remarkable are the Thwa ironsmiths who live among the Himba and make the characteristic Himba throwing spear; and the Zemba and Hakaona tribes who are professional diviners and medicine-men. Traditionally there is barter in beads, shells, iron and copper as well as tobacco and liquor, and now that new and desirable articles of European merchandise are becoming available in the Kaokoveld, many Himba exchange some of their livestock for cash.

Livestock are not only essential for the material well-being of the Himba, they also play a vital role in numerous social and religious ceremonies: bridewealth is always paid in livestock and cattle must be slaughtered at the wedding celebrations. In a man's lifetime he will ritually slaughter cattle, sheep or goats at many special occasions such as name-givings, initiations and funerals. What is more the Himba, like many other African peoples, have a very special relationship with their ancestors to whom they make offerings, usually involving the slaughter of stock, to ensure the continued benevolence of the ancestral spirits.

They have an exceptional knowledge of both animal husbandry and their own harsh environment. Given a single heifer, the Himba herdsman will soon have a flourishing herd. From earliest childhood the boys play games that revolve around the cattle and in this way they learn the Himba's remarkable cattle terminology. By the age of five or six they are out tending the family sheep and goats, often spending many days and nights on their own in the veld so that long before puberty they have learnt independence and

bushcraft. By the time a Himba boy reaches his teens he not only knows all the permanent and seasonal watering-places in his area but is also familiar with the plants on which his cattle feed and those from which medicines can be made for man and beast. His greatest responsibility is, however, to protect his herds and flocks from predators. Sometimes there is direct confrontation, either by chance or during organised hunts in which the heavy throwing spear is used with telling effect. Most of the larger carnivores, however, are nocturnal and therefore more frequently trapped or poisoned. Lion, leopard and hyaena succumb to various natural plant poisons, particularly those the Himba make from species of *Euphorbia, Fockea,* and *Adenium*.

Another distant swirl of dust appears over the plains, this time raised by a flock of goats and sheep following the same route taken earlier by the cattle. Accompanying the flock are three women, five or six children and as many dogs. Bringing up the rear is a single donkey heavily laden with bulging leather and sacking bags to which are also attached a number of large gourds. In addition to the loads on their heads, two of the women carry babies slung on their backs. On reaching the river the flock divides, some joining the cattle at the water trough and the rest browsing on the trees and shrubs. The women, children and dogs move some distance away and settle under a spreading camelthorn. From a skin bag, one of the women takes a few handfuls of small dried raisinlike fruits and shares them out. These *ozombe* are collected in large quantities in April and May when they ripen. They have an exceptionally high sugar content and those not eaten fresh or

174. Where the pale green waters of the Kunene mark the border between Namibia and Angola, the scream of the fish eagle can still be heard.

fermented into a potent drink are dried in the sun and eaten later, either on their own or mixed with maize or other grains when such are available.

Now a small block, the *otjiya,* carved from the soft wood of the *Commiphora glaucescens* and a harder wooden rod, the *ongune,* are unpacked. With a few brisk twirls of the rod in the hole on the block one of the younger men coaxes a few glowing embers down a groove and onto dry litter which is quickly blown in flames. The women busy themselves around the fire, tending the smaller children and repairing the damage to their cosmetics caused by the long dusty walk. All the women are similarly dressed, their naked torsos heavily adorned with necklaces, belts and straps. The most conspicuous item of adornment, however, is the single large white cone-shaped shell worn between the bare breasts. From their hips hang pleated or folded aprons of soft skin, and they wear tightly spiralled copper armlets reaching almost to their elbows. To signify their married status all three wear their hair lengthened with hair shaved from their brothers' heads and fibre into many long thin braids drawn backwards over the shoulders, and on top of their heads perch the characteristic *erembe,* the headdress of marriage. The younger girls wear small skin aprons and a few body decorations. Their hair is in two plaits draped forwards over the face.

The dust has settled and the women resting in the shade blend with the colour of their setting. The bright red sheen of their skin comes from regular smearing with butterfat pigmented with the crushed powder of special oxidised rocks. Added to the mixture are the ground leaves and stems of richly aromatic herbs and, when it is available, the fragrant gum of the Kaokoveld myrrh. The men also annoint themselves using black-tinted fat on the neck and shoulders. Although this cosmetic is much admired it serves a purpose beyond sheer vanity. In the fierce climate it forms a protective layer which helps the body tolerate heat stress and limits dehydration. It also acts as insulation against the cold, enabling the Himba to be out in all weather wearing little more than their customary aprons.

The sun, glowing like a fiery ball, now hangs low in the western sky. The stock have been watered and the two young men stand in the long shadows quietly watching their herds. Near the fire the older men squat on their haunches, talking softly while the women prepare the evening meal of strips of dried goat's meat roasted on the coals, soured milk, and the leaves of a small herb pressed into cakes called *omavanda.*

Today the Himba present a picture of proud affluence as they herd their numerous cattle and considerable flocks in the northern territory. But they have not always been wealthy stock-owners. In fact, less than a century ago there were no cattle in the Kaokoveld and the Himba were destitute refugees. To understand this dramatic change of fortune we must look to their past.

The people who are now called Himba are part of a much larger group of Herero-speaking pastoralists who migrated into what is now Namibia from the north-east, probably some time in the middle of the 16th century. This migration took two routes: the first group crossed the Okavango River and settled in the north where they became known as the Mbanderu; the second group crossed the Kunene and initially settled in the Kaokoveld. When they attempted to move into the better-watered north-east, they were repulsed by the resident Owambo. The only alternative was to look south and about 200 years ago many of them decided to seek fresh pastures and water there. But not all the Herero went south; some elected to remain.

From the start the Kaokoland Herero had adopted an extremely dispersed pattern of settlement, roaming with their cattle between distant watering points and springs. But just as those who had migrated south came into conflict with the pastoralist Nama, so those remaining in Kaokoland in due course fell victim to the marauding Swartbooi and Topnaar Nama bands who had pressed northwards and established a base at Sesfontein. From about 1850 onwards these bands, mounted and equipped with firearms, launched ruthless cattle-raids throughout the north-western territory. The Kaokoland Herero were too widely dispersed to organise any effective resistance and within two decades had lost virtually all their stock. Without their animals many became hunter-gatherers, earning the name of *ovaTjimba.* Some fled back to Angola where they had to beg food from the people there who in turn gave them their present name *ovaHimba* – literally, 'beggars'. But the Himba were not destined to remain poor for long. Soon a remarkable young man was to rescue them from this refugee existence and lead them triumphant back to Kaokoland.

The hero of the Himba return was a young man called Vita, Herero for 'war', and later referred to as 'Oorlog' from the Afrikaans translation. He was the son of a Tswana who had married the sister of a prominent Herero chief, Chief Menassa. While still a youth he decided to follow his father who had accompanied the explorer Frederick Green on an expedition to Angola, and here he encountered the Kaokoland refugees. With little to lose, they were more than prepared to join the militant Vita. Early in 1906 another group of Herero joined Vita in Angola. They were also refugees, this time from the cruel defeat inflicted on the southern Herero by the German forces during the 1904-1907 rebellion. These few hundred men opted to join Vita too, believing that wherever he was, this charismatic young man would ensure them a decent living.

With Vita at their head, the Himba-Herero forces fought many successful campaigns. He had wisely allied himself to the Portuguese colonists in Angola and in return for his assistance in subduing unrest in the south-west of that territory, they supplied him and his followers with rifles and ammunition. During their successful decade at war the Himba accumulated as many cattle as possible, always dividing them among their own people so that those who decided in 1920 to return across the Kunene into Kaokoland once more drove cattle before them.

It is now quite dark and the temperature has dropped considerably; the air is cool. Around the flickering fire the women load the donkey once more while the men and boys disappear in the darkness to gather their herds and flocks. Above the constant lowing and bleating we hear a strange low-pitched whistle and although it is too dark to identify the source, it is clear that the animals are attracted to this sound for they begin to converge from all directions.

The moon is rising now and as we watch a silvery line breaks along the top of the peaks. Within minutes the moon hangs like a great yellow orb over the mountains and valley. In the ghostly light we see the cattle begin to move upriver. In front of them walks a single human figure, at his lips a long oryx horn. The cattle fall silent now and the only sound is the eerie monotonous tooting that fades into the night.

175. Dwarfed by the immensity of the Marienfluss, zebra surge across its sandy wastes.
176. Tjimba men sit talking around a fire in the chill of late evening along the Kunene.

177. The first meal of the day and the inviting aroma of roasted kernels drifts from an open fire.
178. A Tjimba mother and her children.

...oon and two young herders return home. The Himba are
... young men together with their herds race against one
... of manhood.

...dman Waitavira Tjambiru's five wives – her elegant
... of the Himba, and her eyes lowered as a sign of respect.
... are traditionally hunter-gatherers. In contrast to the Himba
... ocky and, as the photograph on the previous page shows,
...atures. However, the two groups have close cultural and
... the latter part of the 19th century when the Herero of the
...attle to marauding Nama and were driven across the
...gola, the Tjimba, too, were affected. They retreated into the

for more than half a century, combing the slopes for wild plant foods,
hunting, and using tools of stone. The Herero who had fled had lost their
only wealth – their cattle – and as refugees became known as ovaHimba,
'beggars', the name they have retained ever since. However, in 1920 the
Himba driving before them the cattle they had plundered during a
successful decade of war, made a proud return to Kaokoland. Gradually the
Tjimba ventured from the mountains and re-established their close
association with the Himba whose language they speak, and whose culture
they share. The principal difference remains economic: the Himba have
become wealthy cattle-owners while the Tjimba still depend largely on
hunting and gathering, although some have managed to acquire herds of

182. Even when eating or sleeping, the Tjimba herder never removes his *orukwe,* a thin brass disc, from his mouth. During the day its shrill whistle cuts the Kaokoland silences and each man's herd rallies to his distinctive call. Metal technology was introduced to the Tjimba only this century, and although they no longer use stone implements, some of these mountain people can still demonstrate how to make and use stone tools.

183. Goats drink from a dam in central Kaokoland.

184. Preparing goat meat over his fire, a young herder waits for a brief summer shower to pass: but even the rain cannot revive the increasingly barren landscape of Kaokoland. In this territory of 50 000 square kilometres the people – estimated at less than 13 000 – have always led a nomadic existence. Water and grazing dictate their movements and only in years of severe drought did they descend from the pastures of the interior to graze the fragile desert grasses of the Pro-Namib. But in the last few decades their herds have increased at such a rate that the highland pastures have been severely overgrazed and drought conditions prevail even in years of normal rainfall. The grasslands have been so damaged that perennials are scarce and the herds must now graze in the Pro-Namib on a regular basis. The outcome is predictable: unless the people of Kaokoland can be induced to limit the size of their herds their territory will eventually become a wasteland.

185. At Waitavira Tjambiru's village the sacred herd mills outside the kraal, waiting to be milked.
186. Another of Waitavira Tjambiru's wives, also annointed from head to foot with butterfat tinted a rich deep ochre. This cosmetic, enhanced by the fragrant gum of the Kaokoveld myrrh, is much admired by the Himba.

185 186

187

188

189

187. A newborn kid draped casually over one hip, a Himba boy stops to share a wild fruit with a friend. The mother goat looks on anxiously. The Himba, like many other Bantu-speaking peoples, keep goats as a source of meat and, from a very young age, the boys are entrusted with their care.

188. Dust hangs heavily about a Himba woman as she moves through the cattle kraal to milk the holy herd at sunrise.

189. No Himba can imagine a meaningful existence without cattle: the size of his herds is his symbol of wealth and status; their milk is a major source of food; they are slaughtered and eaten on ritual occasions such as birth, name-giving, initiation, marriage and, of course, death. This bachelor had trekked these cattle over 200 kilometres in search of fresh grazing. His entire possessions are on the stick he carries and he must trust to his intimate knowledge of his environment to live off whatever the land provides.

190. During funerary rites, which may extend over months, many cattle are slaughtered; in the case of this headman the skulls of some 180 cattle were piled on stakes about his grave reflecting both his wealth and importance. The Himba inherit cattle matrilineally: a man's herds go to his sister's children while his own children inherit from their maternal uncle. However, the eldest son inherits the 'sacred herd' directly from his father, together with the sacred firesticks and, most important of all, custodianship of the sacred fire.

191-193. Deep in contemplation, one of Waitavira Tjambiru's wives pauses (191) before milking her husband's sacred herd (193). Completing this ritual she takes the milk to Tjambiru, seated here beside the sacred fire (192) and, as headman of his lineage he tastes it and pronounces it fit for his kin to drink. The smouldering stump of mopane wood at his feet is never allowed to die: its flame is evidence of his rôle as link between the living and the dead. The ancestor cult is fundamental to the traditional religious beliefs of all the Herero-speaking peoples who believe that their ancestors take an active interest in the lives and well-being of their living kin. What is more, if displeased, the ancestors are believed to be able to bring misfortune and it is the duty of the head of the lineage to maintain contact with them and intervene on behalf of the family members. His keeping alive of the sacred fire underlines this rôle. Should it by mischance die out, he and he alone must relight it with the sacred firesticks. When a headman grows old he usually hands over his

191   192

custodianship of the fire and all it represents to his eldest son; but if he dies unexpectedly, the fire is put out by the mourning relatives and all the symbols of his position are desecrated. The main hut, called 'the place of taboos' in which ritual objects are kept and various ceremonies are performed, is demolished: the special mopane logs kept to feed the fire are destroyed, and the stones at the fire-place are moved around and anyone is free to sit·on them. Every manifestation of the deceased headman's special links with the ancestors is destroyed now that he has become an ancestor himself. The new headman lights a fresh fire with the sacred firesticks he has inherited; then with much ceremony he re-establishes the bonds between the lineage and its past and undertakes the ritual custodianship of the flame.

194. Their contrasting hairstyles immediately indicate the different status of these Himba. The older man assumes the turban of a married man while the youth's head is clean-shaven but for a central panel which he wears long in a single plait.

195

195. Working as a team, Himba collect water from a four metre-deep pit dug in a seemingly dry riverbed at Etengwa.
196. Graceful Hakaona maidens carry water. They are closely related to the Herero-speaking people of southern Angola but a number of families migrated with the Himba to Kaokoland because of the demand for their services as diviners and herbalists.

200. No firelight casts a glow over Himba dances and there is no musical accompaniment but for the compelling handclapping and voices of the women who in turn break into a wild solo and abandon themselves to the ecstasy of dance. Around the neck of this dancing woman hangs a gleaming shell, a prized ornament worn by most Himba women and bartered from people in Angola. She also wears a copper coil around her arm, and on her ankles the bulky iron beads seen on many Himba men and women. The Thwa ironworkers make these beads which they trade for livestock with the Himba. The copper coils are greatly admired items of a Himba matron's finery and she wears them for several months at a time until her skin becomes irritated and she must remove them so that it heals.
201. A woman helps put out a fire begun by accident in the stockade.

202. Headdress of a married woman: the *erembe* of leather perched above her elaborate hair-style. Her own hair is stretched and lengthened with fibre and the entire creation is dressed with a liberal smearing of ochre-tinted butterfat.

203. Headdress of a Themba girl.

204. A bachelor's pigtail which he will wear until he marries in his early twenties.

205. Beaded thongs adorn a young girl's bottom.

206. Intricate belt decorations sported by a Himba youth.

207. Only after marriage do Himba men wear this headdress, traditionally of soft leather covered with pigmented butterfat. This young man sports a cloth turban but like other Himba men he uses an *okati* (stuck behind one ear when not in use) to scratch under his coiffure.

208

209

208, 209. In town, possibly for the first time in their lives, Himba mingle with other Herero-speaking people at a political meeting in Opuwo, capital of Kaokoland. At the meeting they were told something of the changes that would take place when Namibia became independent. Until this meeting many of these Himba men and women – seated separately as tradition dictates – had not conceived of a world outside of their own. Also attending the meeting are Herero, the women in typically colourful attire. The contrast in dress clearly reflects the divergent paths taken by the Himba and Herero who in fact belong to the same nuclear group which entered what is now Namibia from the north some 300 years ago. The Herero who chose to remain in Kaokoland later became known as the 'Himba' and they have clung to their original culture and traditions, accepting change but slowly, and having little contact with more westernised peoples; on the other hand those who migrated further south, now simply called the 'Herero', have been acculturated by peoples such as the Nama and Europeans. Yet they have achieved a remarkable synthesis of old and new and it is this which binds them into the proud and cohesive group they are today.

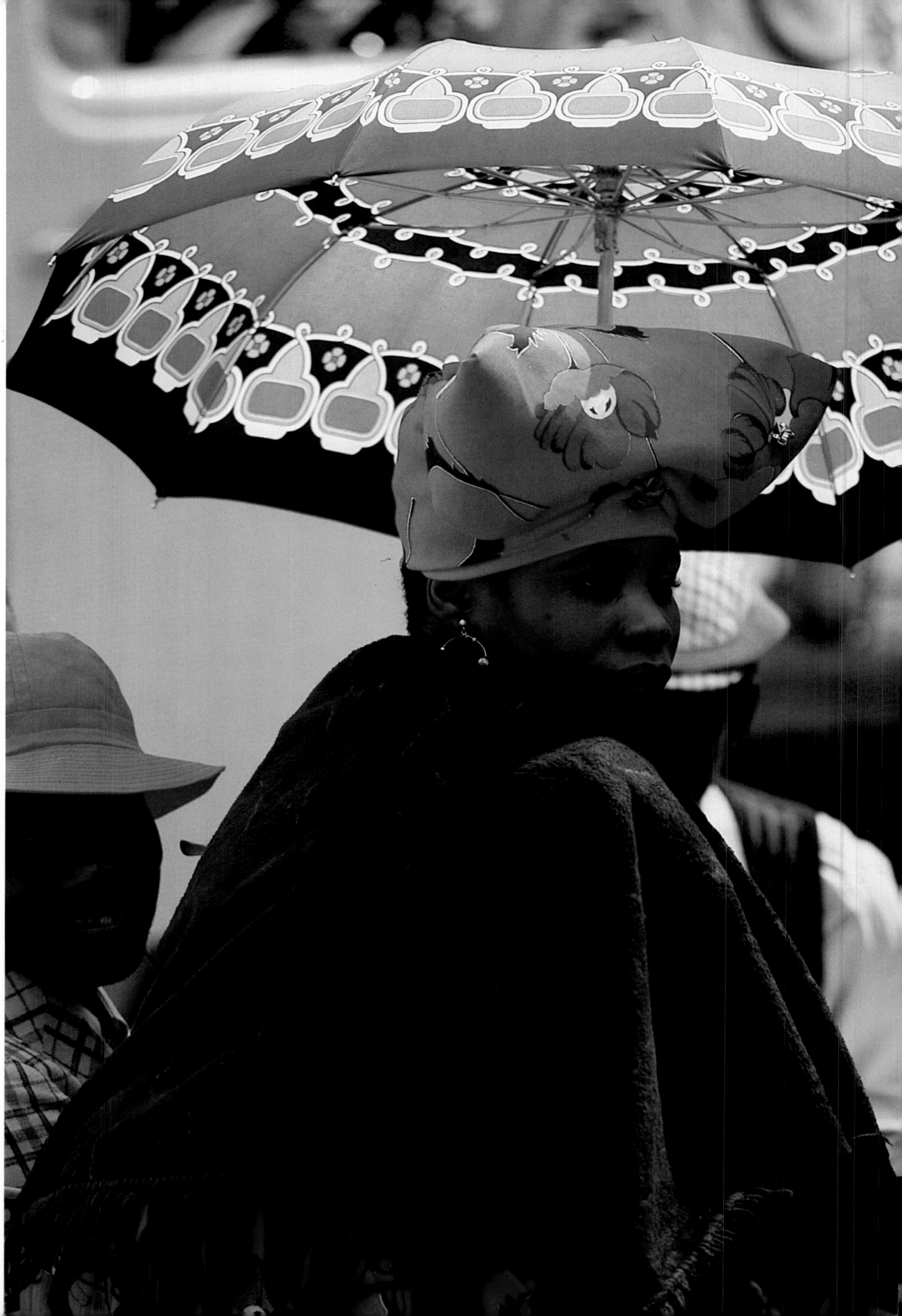

210. Her dress a bold and beautiful extravaganza of colour, a Herero lady shelters under her umbrella. Wherever one goes in Hereroland one sees these women in their magnificent dresses and turbans. The style was originally introduced by the wives of missionaries, anxious to make the local women cover their bodies with more than just ochre and beads: as a result the Herero women adopted the leg o' mutton sleeve, the tightly-buttoned high bodice and fully-gathered skirt, translating these basic elements into a style distinctly their own.
211. This Herero woman had travelled with her baby by bus several hundred kilometres from Windhoek to attend the meeting at Opuwo.
212. Herero women in full regalia gather for a cattle auction at Otjimbingwe.

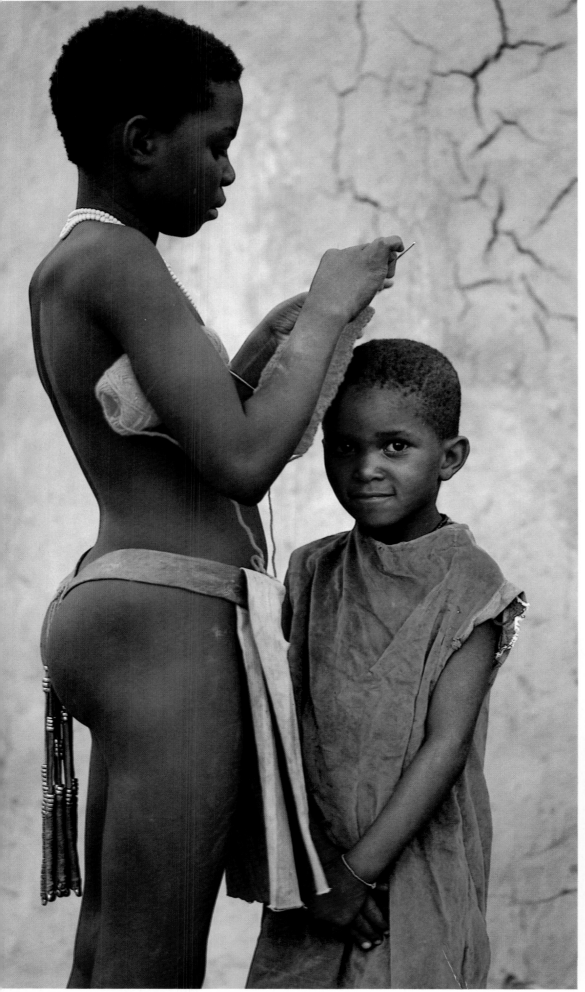

213. A Herero girl knitting a cap for her little sister.
214. Handsome and tall, these Herero women move with a fluid grace.
215. In eastern Kaokoland one can see the transition in style of housing from the traditional Himba 'igloo' to the more westernised Herero hut.
216. Few Herero homes are without a sewing machine. Here a matron sits on the floor of her cool mud and thatch hut and makes herself a typically elaborate dress from cotton cloth bought at the trading store.

213   215

217. A donkey carries two children at Otjimbingwe – its name from the Herero for 'to be refreshed'.
218. Namibia's oldest church, the Lutheran Church at Otjimbingwe – site of one of the earliest mission stations.
219. A Herero child loaded with faggots to cook the evening meal.

220. A feather adds a rakish touch to a Herero stockman's hat.
221. Herero schoolboys set off to school in a donkey cart at Otjimbingwe.
222. Late in the day, a herder drives his cattle to water.

THE BENGUELLA COAST

The inability – and unwillingness – of man to reconcile expectation with reality is historically well-documented. Up until the early 1970s Namibia's Benguella Coast was a case in point, with the optimistic pre-season quotas for pelagic fish as eloquent examples of false expectation and the annually declining catches as reality.

For years the sheer plenitude of this coast blinded those reaping its waters to the dangers of over-exploitation. It is an environment so generous, so fecund, that in terms of the biomass it sustains it has few equals; as a result only recently – and then very slowly – have we begun to appreciate the delicate balance on which this bounty depends. Its source is many thousands of kilometres away in the Antarctic Ocean. From here cold water moves northwards until it submerges beneath the warmer sub-Antarctic waters, becoming a slow, cold, deep-sea river. Gradually, driven by giant oceanic convection systems which are controlled by the winds and ultimately by the sun, this mighty underwater stream of nutrient-rich water moves into a collision course with the southern continents. Deflected by the landmass of Africa, and encouraged to rise to the surface by prevailing winds, it wells up along the west coast of the subcontinent. There it becomes the Benguella Current, teeming womb for the sea-life of Namibia's shores.

For centuries the Strandlopers gathered seafood along this shore and yet did nothing to disturb the grand scheme of things. Zooplankton and phytoplankton bloomed in the photic layer turning the sea into a rich green feeding ground for immense shoals of pilchard and anchovy, maasbanker and mackerel. Nature's fishermen were close behind: gannets plunged from the sky and cormorants dived to swallow their fill; penguins darted underwater on the chase. Among the large predators of the shoals were the Cape fur seals which basked during the breeding season in densely-packed rookeries on the offshore islands and in sheltered bays. At sea the sharks were their enemies and on the mainland the black-backed jackals fought over placentas and sniffed among the newborn pups to weed out the weak and the dying. The solitary strandwolf had a place, too, scavenging the rookeries and loping along the coast in search of scraps tossed up by the surf. Wheeling and screeching above were the gulls, on the look-out for refuse among the seals and for eggs of other seabirds in the great breeding colonies.

Then in 1948 man the profiteer, super-predator of all, discovered the feast of fish. He has proved in many ways an unwelcome guest, and without doubt a foolish one. His greed has thrown into jeopardy the well-being of all the others who for so long shared the bounty of this sea.

European voyagers had seen the potential of the Benguella Coast long before they recognised the wealth of the land itself. By the late-1700s English and American whalers and sealers were operating out of what were to become Luderitz and Walvis (Whale) Bay. The first chapter in the story of over-exploitation belongs to them. With little inkling that their pursuit of the whale would one day threaten its very existence, they set up settlements to process the carcases. Today their rusting blubber pots lie discarded on the beaches among huge bleached bones.

During the many years when these men hunted here their lives must have been as bleak as their surroundings. The ripe smell of flensed carcases was heavy in the daily shroud of fog, there was a shortage of fresh water, a shortage of women, and little to inspire them in the task at hand – but the belief that the sea would be forever abundant.

The second chapter belongs to the era of 'white gold', the immense guano deposits discovered on the numerous offshore islands. Here gannets, cormorants and penguins nested in their thousands, depositing layer upon layer of pungent nitrate-rich guano. In 1828 Captain Benjamin Morrell, an American involved in the oil and seal industry along the Benguella Coast, wrote an account of his voyages and reported that he had seen islands covered in guano eight metres thick. Few read his account and those who did saw little in it – Europe and America had yet to realise the value of guano as a fertiliser. But in the late 1830s shipments from Peru reached Europe and speculators and entrepreneurs quickly recognised the possibilities of similar deposits elsewhere.

First to reach the African prize was Andrew Livingstone of Liverpool. He had read Morrell's report, and with much secrecy raised capital for an expedition south. But the news soon leaked out and by 1843 the Great Guano Rush was on. Guano collecting was not attractive work but it promised magnificent returns. 1844 and 1845 were years of hysteria and violence as 6 000 men, described by the explorer Charles Andersson as 'the lowest order of humanity', battled to wrest a share. In that two-year period, guano worth £2 000 000 was removed. Rarely has a natural resource been so ruthlessly exploited – and so quickly. By 1855 the islands were all but stripped.

Plumpudding, Possession, Hollamsbird, Halifax, Ichaboe, Pomona and the other islands are generally low and featureless. There is scant rainfall to leach the guano and year after year the gannets build their nests from old deposits, but by harvesting the guano down to bedrock man has reduced the suitability of many of the traditional breeding grounds. If gannets were prejudiced by human activities, cormorants – by virtue of numbers, the largest guano producers – found in man a benefactor.

The idea of building platforms along the coast to attract seabirds to roost, breed – and deposit guano – dates back to the early years of this century. The prototype, Bird Rock platform, was built in 1930 and was an immediate success. In ever-increasing numbers Cape cormorants took to the platform which was gradually enlarged. The Cape cormorant does not require guano for nest-building and after each breeding season the guano is systematically removed for commercial purposes. Several of these platforms have been built and the exercise is profitable but not extravagantly so: in years when the fish are poor many birds do not breed and the guano deposits are disappointing.

Commercial fishing is another complicating factor in the fine balance of the ecology of this coast. Fishing off Namibia's shores has developed into a major industry only in the last three decades since the necessary technology – for canning and also for processing fish-meal and fish-oil – became available. The fish stocks appeared to be enormous, the shoals homogeneous, and purse seiners put out to sea. The years between 1950 and 1960 were ones of stability. Quotas were set, controlled and filled: expectation burgeoned and for once it appeared that reality was not far behind. Canneries and reduction plants producing fish-meal and fish-oil were set up at Walvis Bay while Luderitz developed as a centre of the rock lobster – and diamond – industries. Investors saw this as an opportunity not equalled since the Great Guano Rush and they were determined to take as much as they could.

From the early 1960s signs of future instability were apparent to those able to read the signs, but greed prevailed in other quarters and more and more concessions and quotas were awarded. Yet, while euphoria gripped the industry, researchers were making sober assessments. They had begun systematic studies of the way in which the many factors along this coast interact. But while they examined the marine environment, observed the life-cycles of the shoals, and counted bird and seal populations from aerial photographs, the investors gloated over figures that in 1968 promised enormous wealth. In that season a million and a half tons of pilchard alone were pumped from the boats.

That was the high point. Since then the graph has followed a downward trend. In 1970 the nets were empty and panic gripped the industry. Yet despite the panic and despite the evident scarcity of fish, quotas remained optimistic – even though they were split so that pilchard catches were limited and the emphasis placed on alternative pelagic species such as anchovy.

Initially the industry lashed out at others – foreign trawlers were invading their waters, and the birds and Cape fur seals were taking too much. The seals were cause for concern, not so much for the quantities of fish they consumed but as a disruptive influence. Behind every purse seiner came a flotilla of seals, and by the time the crew had fixed their sonar and echo sounder on their source of livelihood, the seals had discovered the shoal, too, and were off in pursuit, dispersing the fish before the net could be deployed. If a shoal was already captured they frightened the catch which might then escape through the bottom or back of the net. Their frenzied feeding sometimes even caused the catch to sound and capsize the boat by the force of its panic, while the seals could always shred the net to escape.

Although there is controlled culling of the substantial seal colonies along the coast, this does not solve the problems of fishermen on the job. Various proposals have been put forward for keeping the seals away from the nets and underwater transmitting devices may be the most humane. Calls of the killer whale were used in initial experiments but the seals did not respond as anticipated. Work continues on specially developed electronic devices.

The seals are but one factor in the overall problem. In years when there are abnormalities in the environment such as higher water temperatures and possibly the lack of upwelling of nutrient-rich water in the Benguella Current, their body oil yields show that the fish are in poor condition. What is more, fewer seabirds breed which indicates that food is not plentiful. These are warning signs that the eggs and larvae may not have a high rate of survival which would affect future prospects. It also appears that quotas should be readjusted to a lower level in years when there are relatively few fish and conditions are bad. Not to do so is to court disaster. Indeed, had the environment not obliged and the conditions of 1967/68 been particularly good for egg and larval survival, those halcyon years might well have sounded the death knell

224. Locked in eternal conflict, the sea and sand of Namibia's dread Skeleton Coast. At night jackals fill the air with their eerie howling and by day the south-westerly winds whip sand along the dreary beaches.
225. Plankton-rich foam trails along the shore where a wreck lies buried.
226. As the Atlantic surf pounds on the rocks, a breeding colony of Cape fur seals mass along a remote beach of the Sperrgebiet. In October each year the bulls lumber ashore to win their territories and establish their harems. A few weeks later the cows give birth and after seven days they come on heat and mating begins. Many of the young perish beneath the hulking bodies of the bulls eager to copulate. The fertilised ovum will lie dormant within the womb for four months and only then does the eight-month gestation period begin. Many of the cows remain close to the colony all year round, tending their young; the bulls, free of responsibility, take once more to the sea.

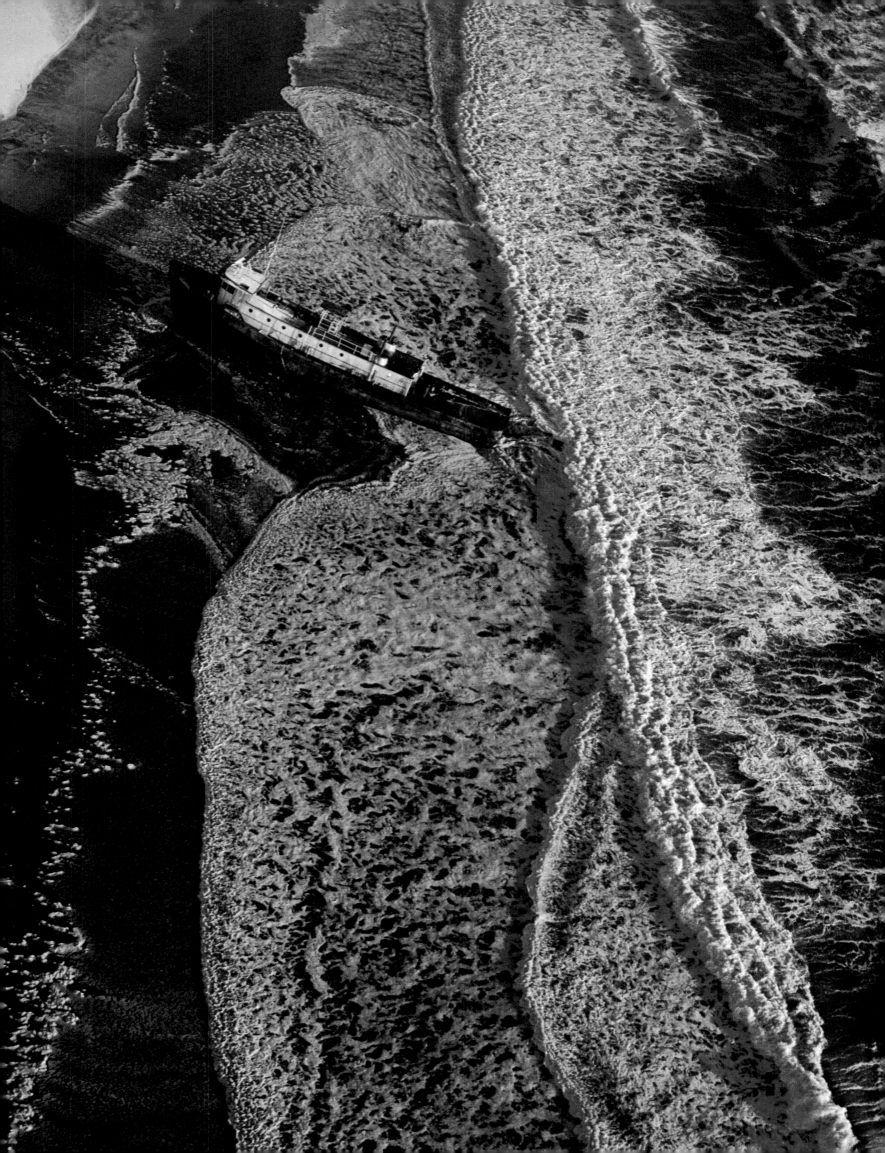

of Namibia's pilchard industry. As it was, four years later in 1971 the nets were all but empty.

After mining, the sea provides Namibia with its second greatest source of foreign exchange. With careful management it will yield the country with invaluable protein into the infinite future, but even the Benguella Coast has its limits. The marine ecosystem, be it seal, seagull, strandwolf, fish or man's activities must be monitored, for to disturb the balance by damaging any one is to prejudice the others. Man will have to learn how to reap what Nature offers without destroying the abundance which the waters of the Benguella Coast provide.

227. A Cape fur seal pup slips from the womb. Freed of the foetal sac it suckles within the hour and by the time it is six weeks old will be able to swim strongly.
228. Only a day old and already inquisitive, this pup is called back by its anxious mother.
229. Deceptively languid, a bull keeps a watchful eye on the zealous bachelors who, without harems of their own, are perpetually on the lookout for a willing female.

227 229
228

230. Black-backed jackal contest a dead seal pup. These predators move freely through the colony, seeking out as their prey the weak and dying young.

231. Three protagonists in the huge breeding colonies: the seal, the jackal, unchallenged as it moves through the rookery scavenging placentas and dead and dying pups, and the gull which comes for the pickings.

232. The entire ecology of this coast begins with the nutrient-rich Benguella Current. Here in the cold waters plankton blooms and immense shoals of pilchard, maasbanker and anchovy feed. Close behind come the seals and the birds. Here a throng of jackass penguins move through the breakers in search of squid and the gleaming shoals along Namibia's fecund coast.

233. Crayfish boats off the coast near Luderitz – centre of the lucrative 'rock lobster' industry.

234. Gannets plunge headlong with wild abandon into waters teeming with maasbanker.

235. As the sun hangs low in the sky, cormorants return to roost on a guano platform. There are several of these man-made platforms along the coast and they are the basis of the present-day guano industry. The prototype, Bird Island, was built in 1930 amid much scepticism. Yet within minutes of completion of the original section, the first cormorants descended. Since then the Bird Island platform has been continually enlarged and after the breeding season the year's accumulation of guano is collected. In the background lie supertankers riding at anchor awaiting commission. Since the rise in oil prices cut demand, at least ten of these vessels lie redundant off Namibia's coast.

236. Far from home waters, a Norwegian fisherman under contract to a fishing company helps pack the net onto the deck of a purse seiner operating off the Skeleton Coast.

237. Skipper Derek van Rensburg watches anxiously as the net is hauled in. Since the early seventies the pilchard catches have declined and the fishermen are forced to set their nets for catches of maasbanker and anchovy.

238. Maasbanker, anchovy and snoek fill the hold of a purse seiner returning to the processing factory.

239. At 03:00 hours on a bitterly cold morning, men pump anchovies from the deck of a trawler overflowing with fish. This catch will be processed into fish-meal – far less profitable than canned pilchards.

236 237
238 239

THE SPERR-GEBIET

The long passage of geological time has twisted Namibia's fabled Diamond Coast into today's gaunt desert shore. Here, in the southern marches of the country, the Orange River, grey-brown with silt, comes down from the Richtersveld mountains and empties into the sea at Oranjemund. And here, on prehistoric beach terraces north of the Orange River estuary are the richest gem diamond deposits known to man. These diamonds, stones of superb quality, are mined in massive and dramatic operations, often in the face of the violent hard-running surf of the south Atlantic.

This area is part of the *Sperrgebiet* – 'the forbidden region' – where, under the German administration at the beginning of the century, prospecting and mining were exclusively reserved for the Deutsche Kolonial Gesellschaft für Südwest-Afrika, and they have remained under the control of the country's administration ever since. Casual and unauthorised visitors do not come to know the Diamond Coast.

In this compelling setting of almost menacing beauty the romance and legendry of diamonds takes on a new dimension. The Sperrgebiet has an allure born of desolation and a humbling sense of all-pervading age. As mining uncovers the gullied pre-Cambrian bedrock from beneath the desert sands, you feel that you have glimpsed the far edges of Time itself.

The diamonds on this coast came from far away and long ago, tribute to the ocean from the whole subcontinent of Africa. Weathered from numerous volcanic pipes, more than a hundred million years old, they were gathered by an ancient river network – the prehistoric Orange and its tributaries, some of them still flowing but most no more than fossil riverbeds. This system tapped areas of major modern diamond production – Kimberley in South Africa, Orapa and Twaneng in Botswana and Letseng-la-Terai in Lesotho. A fossil tributary system of the Orange drained what is today Bushmanland where many kimberlite pipes, barren now but not necessarily so then, have been discovered.

This great central drainage system gathered a rich bounty of diamonds which were stored in the deepening river gravels for the next stage of their epic journey to the sea. But, as yet, the Orange River did not reach the ocean: it ended, most geologists believe, in a vast pan-like area inland of the coastal escarpment.

Then about 70 million years ago new forces were let loose. A period of upheaval elevated the land, increasing the rate of flow of the rivers and in turn the rate of erosion. The Orange burst through the eastern escarpment to the Atlantic, cutting a channel to which it has clung ever since. Over a period, in a huge scouring operation, it took with it most of the accumulated gravels. A first great pulse of diamonds went down to the sea and where the river met the ocean it began depositing its gravels in what ultimately became an immense submarine delta. Over millions of years the sea, advancing and withdrawing with the fluctuations of the great northern ice ages, worked and reworked the diamonds, concentrating them dramatically and also, by chemical action and the physical pounding of the violent seas, destroying and removing those of poor quality. What was left were gem diamonds of incomparable quality. And these were distributed in the ocean; the largest near the river mouth and the smaller stones further up and down the coast where stormy surf, in major sea invasions and retreats, deposited them with gravels and small boulders in the gullies of the ocean bedrock and in layers on beaches which are up to 3 500 metres from the present shoreline.

241 242
243

Then, about two million years ago, the land rose again and the second and most recent pulse of river gravels and diamonds reached the delta of the Orange, where the whole long process of concentration and distribution was repeated. This period saw the formation of the ancient beach terraces which are mined today along the Oranjemund coast, but not of the Luderitz deposits where the first diamond finds were made. These were much older and related to the first great spasm of the Orange River, and to a very high stand of sea.

Between the Orange River and Affenrucken, the 100 kilometres of coast covered by the mining activity of CDM (Consolidated Diamond Mines of South West Africa), there are six major marine terraces reflecting a succession of ancient sea invasions, each followed by a major withdrawal. The older three – perhaps up to a million years in age – have been formed against a well-defined sea cliff cut into the bedrock. At their highest these beaches are now 25 metres above sea level. This older or upper group has a distinctive calcrete layer above the gravels and all three possess a fossil fauna, now either extinct or occurring only in warmer waters. The younger raised beaches, nearer the present shore, could be about 120 000 years old. They have a modern cold-water fauna.

Contrary to earlier opinions, the diamonds were not carried up this coast by the cold, north-flowing Benguella Current: its speed of four to five knots is not sufficient to carry heavier material for many kilometres up the coast. The moving force was the long shore drift caused by the strong prevailing winds, south-west for nine-tenths of the year and north-west for the remainder, which have helped the sea deposit a long trail of diamonds north of the river and for a much shorter distance to the south.

And so, over millions of years, the elements have conspired to build up a vast treasure trove on these lonely beaches, and it has taken Man a mere half century to fathom Nature's secrets and expose the limits of the diamond trail.

241. The Orange River flows diamond-bright from the Richterveld Mountains to the distant coast at Oranjemund.
242. Alone with his mirror image, a stilt treads a fog-blurred tidal pool at Oranjemund.
243. Agate, jasper, amazonite, carnelian lie between a surf-tumbled gleam of pebbles on the Diamond Coast.

MEMORIES OF A GHOST TOWN Marianne Coleman recalls an all but forgotten era:

'I was born in Pomona, South West Africa, in 1917. My mother was German and my father was of Danish/German descent. He was an engineer and like all the people who lived in what are now the ghost towns he worked for 'the Company' – after 1920 called Consolidated Diamond Mines of South West Africa but referred to affectionately by those who worked for them as 'the Co.'

It is not surprising that one of my earliest childhood memories is of diamonds for at Pomona they found the most beautiful gems. I remember the labourers being sent out in the morning with an empty jam jar, a small brush and a shovel, and returning later in the day, the jars blazing with diamonds they had swept out of indentations in the rock.

The house I was born in still stands there today: it may need a few window panes and a good sweeping out, but you could live in it again. It was built high on a hill where the sandstorms swept past it and it was so solid that the elements have done very little harm. I went back last year before I retired and I felt like a ghost wandering through the rooms. Sand drifts piled high in the corners and thin shafts of pale sunlight cut through the dusty air. I revisited the offices, the Post Office, the workings, and found it difficult to believe that all is gone and done with. Perhaps one day they will go back and find more diamonds, who knows. In its heyday Pomona was alive with people, it even sported a skittle alley for, as you know, the Germans always built a skittle alley before anything else. It was their favourite form of relaxation. The skittle alley at Pomona was so delightful and well-made that it was later removed to Oranjemund where it is still in use.

When the workings finally stopped, Pomona became a half-way station for the Company bus between Luderitz and Oranjemund. Everyone who came away from Oranjemund had to be X-rayed to check if diamonds were being smuggled out. In those days it was strip to the bone, everyone was handed a sheet and you were left to your own devices until it was your turn to get on that cold marble slab and be X-rayed. Still, it was fun and if the wind did play havoc with the sheets, no one worried.

When I was a little older we moved to Kolmanskop. It had been founded in 1908 when a coloured man, who was working for Mr Stauch who was building the railway to Keetmanshoop, found a few diamonds in the sand. Mr Stauch was not sure if they were diamonds so he took them to Luderitz for expert opinion. When it was discovered that they were the real thing, the rush was on. Hundreds of small companies were formed and Luderitz became a boom town. Kapps Hotel became the Stock Exchange and lucky barmaids were paid in diamonds when cash ran out. Like most boom towns, Luderitz was short of women and some of the barmaids went on to marry very well.

We lived at Kolmanskop from 1922, by which time CDM had been formed. The entire company was run by Germans, from the General Manager down, and at one time there were only two English-speaking families living there.

Even today, when the houses stand deserted and silent while the sand gradually sifts through and over them, it is incredible to see what was achieved. Of course in my time the sand was removed every day by Owambos who collected up the drifts from the day before and carried them off to be dumped outside the town.

In my photograph album there is a picture of the first wedding at Kolmanskop and I was flowergirl, overdressed in European style despite the desert climate. The reception was held in the old corrugated iron 'casino' which was replaced by the new recreation hall. They brought out a man from Germany to design the hall for perfect acoustics and he did such an excellent job that even now when visiting choirs enter the recreation hall they cannot resist breaking into song. I well remember dances and shows in this very hall. They were lavish and every sophisticated taste was catered for. Once they turned the entire club into a ship – the stage was the Captain's bridge where only champagne was served, the cabins were little coffee bars, liqueur bars and so on. While the wind whipped sand across the windows we were able to choose between two dining places: along one side of the hall was a choice of delicacies such as salmon, caviar and paté, while along the other was served rough seaman's food like pea soup, pork and sauerkraut. This particular dance went on for three days and on Monday when the hooter blew for everyone to get back to work, the last stragglers turned up with their sailor's caps still on. I remember another of these occasions when they transformed the hall into a Japanese scene and I must add that Germans dressed up as Japanese look pretty jolly. These affairs, which were always in aid of charity, usually ended up at our house to the sound of the old wind-up gramophone. There would be cold champagne and all sorts of things to eat. We really enjoyed ourselves.

The mine also brought out from Europe opera companies, theatre groups and orchestras for our entertainment. We had an active theatre group of our own and a local orchestra which played at thé dansants every Saturday and Sunday afternoon. These were great fun and people came all the way from Luderitz to attend.

The butcher, the baker and the general dealer's store were all run by the mine; so was the ice-making factory which also made delicious lemonade and soda water. Every morning, a block of ice to fit into the ice-box in your home was delivered free of charge. One of these old-fashioned ice-boxes can still be seen in the Kolmanskop skittle alley.

The hospital at Kolmanskop stands out in my memory – and so do the two doctors. Dr Kraenzle believed that all convalescing patients should have a few caviar sandwiches washed down by a half-bottle of champagne every evening. The other doctor was a bone specialist who not only believed that you should eat a raw onion every day if you wanted to stay healthy, but that you should whistle while you ate it! He was a weird and wonderful figure in the village, but it was an assault on the senses to be examined by him unless, in self-defence, you too ate an onion beforehand. I also recall that the hospital boasted the finest X-ray machine in the whole of southern Africa. When Kolmanskop was finally closed down, this machine was carefully packed up and sent as a present to Owamboland where our labourers and house servants came from. The hospital is deserted now and wind and sand have taken their toll, but the wine cellar is still there for all to see.

Another relic is the swimming bath on the hill. It was just a square of even depth and although it is now half-filled with sand you can still see the Italian terrazzo tiles. The water was pumped in continuous flow 35 kilometres from Elizabeth Bay and afterwards was used on the mine.

Although we were deep in the desert we had a Post Office and a school up to Standard 3. There is a picture of me all dressed up for school. We didn't wear uniforms as it is not the German custom but there I am in dirndl dress and long woollen stockings to protect my legs from the stinging sand.

Life for the children on the mine was marvellous. There were swings and merry-go-rounds in the playground and no

245-248. Less than half a century has passed since people 'lived, laughed and loved' in this desert town. Today sand sifts over and through the memories and the relics of their past.

245 246
247 248

249. One of several Second World War tanks converted by Consolidated Diamond Mines during earlier mining operations to remove the massive overburden that conceals the diamond-rich gravels.
250. Wild horses freely roam the desert, grazing the sparse grasses and drinking at a specially maintained waterhole.

249 250

one who grew up there will forget the Easter parties the Company arranged for us. Chocolate eggs and rabbits were hidden in coloured straw among the beautiful blue dolomite stones and we knew, with the trusting faith of little children, that the Easter Bunny lived in the desert. After we had found our eggs we were given as many cakes and sweets as we could decently eat. Even as children life was sweet. You had no worries – everything was done for you.

Now that the desert has taken over it is difficult to believe that there were beautiful gardens, both inside and out. There was no shortage of water and our own garden had four large eucalyptus trees, roses and a lawn. Only the stumps of the trees – and my photograph album – remain as my witness. Our indoor garden was beautiful, too, and the walls were painted to match the flowers. My mother's pride and joy, the hand-painted designs on the dining room walls, now a little faded, are even more elegant than they were when the German artist brought out for this purpose originally made them. Tea-parties were usually held here and all the ladies vied with one another, making their houses as attractive as they could. When the German boats called at Luderitz the local ladies made a special trip to buy lilies-of-the-valley and other typically European flowers from the ship. And as soon

as they returned home they would place their new potted plants in pride of place in the indoor garden. These small things took on such importance when you lived in the desert.

Our power came from Luderitz which had, at the time, the largest power station in southern Africa, and fresh water came in by rail in great torpedoes from Garub, 120 kilometres away. It was first pumped into storage tanks and then piped to the houses.

It was difficult to keep pets in the desert but one family had an ostrich which pulled a sleigh over the sand. An ostrich is not a docile beast and this one was the terror of Kolmanskop. Nevertheless the sleigh was used at Christmas-time to bring Father Christmas. It stands today in the small museum at Kolmanskop where you can also see the old cobbler's bench, the sewing machine and the old-fashioned mangles from the laundry.

Kolmanskop is deserted, but those who lived there have never forgotten it and no matter where they live they always come back. They wander through the museum, touching, feeling, remembering; and as they walk through the deserted houses in the darkening gloom of dusk a shiver of fear may pass through them as they remember that there were once people here – living, loving and laughing.'

LEGACY OF DIAMONDS With the discovery of diamonds at Luderitz in 1908 it seemed almost as if Man were prying: suddenly the majestic tempo of earth's history was interrupted by the feverish activities surrounding a chance discovery of diamonds – the scramble for licences, the frenzy of speculation, land deals and diamond rushes.

From this time on man became the director of events in the unfolding drama of the Namib diamonds – in their prospecting, mining and marketing – yet always seeming just a little out of place, always something of an intruder in the secret enclaves of the desert.

Diamond discoveries in the 1860s in the Kimberley region of South Africa had created a widespread awareness of these glittering gems – and the possibility of other exciting finds in southern Africa. It was therefore not altogether surprising that the man who first stumbled upon diamonds in Namibia and recognised them for what they were should earlier have worked at Kimberley. The exact day is not recorded but the find occurred some time in April 1908. The year before, August Stauch had become permanent-way inspector for a section of railway line running inland from Luderitz, through Aus to Keetmanshoop, and he had warned his workers to keep their eyes open for unusual stones.

He did not have long to wait before one of his men, Zacharias Lewala, who had earlier worked for De Beers at Kimberley, was shovelling drift sand near the tracks at Kolmanskop – the first station out of Luderitz – when he uncovered several stones he suspected were diamonds. He handed them in and Stauch had his hopes confirmed; they were indeed the real thing.

This discovery triggered a diamond rush in this region, and very soon a spectacular concentration of gems had been found lying in the windswept valleys parallel to the sea. They had come, geologists said later, from ancient marine gravel beds established far inland during a very high stand of sea some 70 million years ago, and later broken down by storms and exposure. The scouring winds had amassed the diamonds on the valley floors while simultaneously removing a greater part of the sand overburden.

The early prospectors did not initially associate the diamonds with the sea. The raised beach deposits of the Orange River region, which were to prove richer still, remained hidden for another 20 years. But the gems littered over the barren valley floors south of Luderitz were considered the richest deposits in the world at the time and they created a colourful, if somewhat bizarre, moment in the story of Namibia's diamonds.

Here, in the early days, the gems were picked off the surface by hand. Hundreds of workers, muffled against the sand-laden wind, would slowly cross a valley floor on their hands and knees, collecting diamonds in little jam tins. And when one of the first discoveries was made just before dark, the frenzied search continued late into the night, the glitter of diamonds reflected by moonlight. This was a boom time for Luderitz and its tiny harbour. Out in the desert ornate residences were built to express the new prosperity and

within them evolved a life style at once unique and fabulous. But the 1914 War interrupted this flamboyance and for a period diamond recovery came to a halt.

The end of the war saw a new phase in the story of the Sperrgebiet. In 1920 Sir Ernest Oppenheimer, then emerging as a leading figure in the world of diamonds, entered into lengthy negotiations with the nine German diamond companies in South West Africa. The outcome was the formation of the Consolidated Diamond Mines of South West Africa (CDM) – one of the companies in the De Beers Group – which now operates from Oranjemund with its head office at Windhoek. CDM continued to operate for several years in the Luderitz field, but the deposits were slowly being depleted and by the thirties the area was in a decline. Soon places such as Pomona, Elizabeth Bay, Bogenfels and Kolmanskop became ghost towns, the excitement, the ostentation of the diamond field and its whole surge of life no more than memories. The entire focus of the industry now moved to the southern edge of the Namib.

German prospectors had for some time been ranging far down the coast from Luderitz to the Orange River and in one of the ironies of history a Dr Reuning in 1910 arranged the digging of a few prospecting pits in the north bank river gravels – without result. These pits, rediscovered in 1928, were only 60 metres from the rich marine deposits subsequently found in the area.

Prospecting in this region increased in tempo in the 1920s and in 1927 Dr Hans Merensky, the brilliant and intuitive geologist who had noted the presence of ancient oyster shells in the gravels in one of the boreholes south of the river, deduced that these gravels were deposited by the sea. At last geologists were on the trail and it was not long before the first diamond-bearing marine terrace at Alexander Bay had been discovered.

These significant finds south of the Orange River mouth drew CDM's attention to the coast immediately north of the river and here even more extensive diamond-bearing marine terraces were found. The world depression of the early 1930s inhibited mining plans, however, and it was not until 1936, when the town of Oranjemund was established, that mining in the area was intensified. The Second World War affected operations to some extent, but at the beginning of the 1950s with the building of the Oppenheimer Bridge across the Orange River, major exploitation of the marine deposits of the Diamond Coast began.

Since then the mining story has been one of increasingly massive mechanisation and technical sophistication.

The mining operation at CDM is simple in concept: the overburden of desert sand, sometimes 12 to 15 metres thick, must be removed to reveal the fossil beach deposits, the marine gravels and the schist bedrock on which the gems lie. But if the principle is simple, the execution is not. The complicating factor is its size, the immense scale of the mechanical operations. Gone are the days of diamonds on the sand for the taking: the proportion of overburden removed to diamonds recovered is now about 200 million to one. To shift about 50 million tons of overburden a year CDM uses some 300 earthmoving machines including scrapers, bulldozers, front-end loaders, rear dump-trucks, and a bucket-wheel excavator in one of the biggest continuous earth-moving operations in the world. But while mechanisation accomplishes the giant's share of the undertaking, the final act in this diamond-mining scenario belongs to an earlier epoch; mine workers, tiny figures moving slowly across the colossal man-made stage,

251. On calm days the majestic scale of the Sperrgebiet becomes breathtakingly apparent: the vast southern Atlantic, neither still nor placid but heaving from below like a deep-breathing giant, guards and simultaneously threatens the Diamond Coast. From the mouth of the Orange River silt streaks north along the coast fringed with great white rollers. From the beach the grey desert marches away in dunes to the escarpment, smoke purple, and at the estuary, Oranjemund with its population of 8 000 seems to cling to the river for comfort.

hand-sweep the bedrock gullies to recover the gems trapped there by the sea long ago.

There is another area of mining in the Sperrgebiet besides the raised beach terraces above sea level: the shoreline between high and low water mark. For some years diamonds were mined at sea as well, out beyond the surf, from specially designed mining barges served by helicopter. This did not prove payable and work stopped but prospecting on the seabed with a new exploration vessel continues.

Around the same time operations from the shore were extended to the beach below the high-water mark, and this aspect of CDM's activities makes the most dramatic visual impact of the immensity of the undertaking of diamond recovery along this desert coast. Simply stated, the beach mining consists of clearing the sand overburden from the area and pushing millions upon millions of tons into the surf, so altering the profile of the beach and forcing the sea back some 200 metres. Sea walls of sand, ten metres high and 15 metres wide, are piled up to form paddocks each 100 metres long. Behind them, with the sea held back and vacuum pumps connected to well-points keeping the wall and excavation relatively dry, mining continues down to bedrock – in some cases 20 metres below mean sea level.

During the frequent storms along this coast the surf attacks the sand walls and part of the mining effort, which continues by night under ghostly floodlights, is to maintain the barricade in the face of the ferocious pounding of the surf. Often an emergency call goes out for more men and machines to hold back the sea: everyone is conscious of the disastrous effect of losing a mining paddock to a break-in of the sea, besides the wasted effort there is the loss of costly equipment under several metres of sea.

The mining of the raised fossil beach deposits is basically the same as the modern foreshore mining – without the sea walls. A wide prospecting trench is driven across the face of the deposit, and where the conglomerate is stubborn it is drilled and blasted loose. The final operation is the careful sweeping of the bedrock gullies.

Material from mining operations in the Sperrgebiet is crushed and concentrated at four primary treatment plants, one in each mining area. From here the material is sent to the central recovery plant for final concentration and delivery to the 'sort-house', where X-rays are used to detect the presence of diamonds and separate them from the waste.

The sorting house is about five kilometres from Oranjemund, the administrative and executive heart of the Diamond Coast operations. The town, blessed with the waters of the Orange River, defies the desert: hibiscus, bougainvillea, grape vines, oleanders and olives flourish alongside roses, daisies and pansies in the shelter of high garden walls and the surrounding acacia and macrocarpa windbreaks. Sparrows hop on watered suburban lawns in contrast to the flamingoes and the pelicans which feed on the yacht club pan just outside the town, and the thousands of cormorants which fly over at day's end to rest on sandbanks in the estuary; in striking contrast, as well, to the jackal, the strandwolf and the honey badger, which make the desert their home but come to drink at the water pipes beyond the town boundaries, and the beautiful oryx, which sometimes wanders along the coast.

Oranjemund is also the home at any one time of some 5 000 Owambo and Kavango workers who come from the far plains of Owamboland and Kavangoland (1 600 kilometres to the north) to the mine for an average of eight months. A

252. A diamond of approximately two carats still embedded in the limestone conglomerate.
253. Known as 'bedrock sweepers', these men shovel the last of the sand from the bedrock which they will then scour by hand and brush for gems hidden in the crevices.
254, 255. Along the Diamond Coast is the biggest fleet of privately owned earth-moving equipment in the southern hemisphere. Night and day these machines work to remove the sands that overlie the diamond-rich gravels.

special relationship has existed between Owambos and CDM for over half a century. Originally they came to work for the German mining companies in the Luderitz area, and what might be called the 'Owambo connection' was inherited by CDM. These men have contributed much to the special human fabric which has, over the eventful years, been woven at Oranjemund. And when they return north and sit around their homestead fires often the conversation will turn to *popia sidema* – 'talking CDM'.

'Talking CDM' is also a feature of any gathering of the international community on the mine, and shop-talk is readily provoked – discussions on mining methods, on geology and the origin of the diamonds, and on attempts at smuggling. The most dramatic story is of a CDM prospector who stored a valuable cache of diamonds deep in the desert. He then travelled to Cape Town and found a pilot prepared to risk the crime. They flew to the Diamond Coast, landing on the remote stretch of beach near the cache. But the prospector had miscalculated the tides: the beach was sodden, the sand yielding, and the aircraft bogged down soon after landing. Shortly afterwards the men were arrested, with the diamonds. The aircraft was confiscated and for some years stood on dis-

play at Oranjemund, a monument to failure – and a warning.

But even the crimes and the attempted crimes have a quality of excitement and grandeur about them which is in keeping with the saga of the coastal gems. And nowhere is this mystique more apparent than in the display, spread out on one large table at the Oranjemund sorting house, of a day's production – about 5 000 carats. Here in every shape and fiery colour is a sight to enchant, a sight perhaps to inflame, a sight certainly to remember – gemstones from an ancient world, recovered by modern methods, in what is one of the most unusual mining operations in the world today.

256. Part of a day's production, diamonds on the sorting table at Oranjemund's main recovery plant.
257. The lights of No. 4 Plant at Oranjemund.
258. An aerial perspective transfigures a salt works into an abstract etched in brown and white.

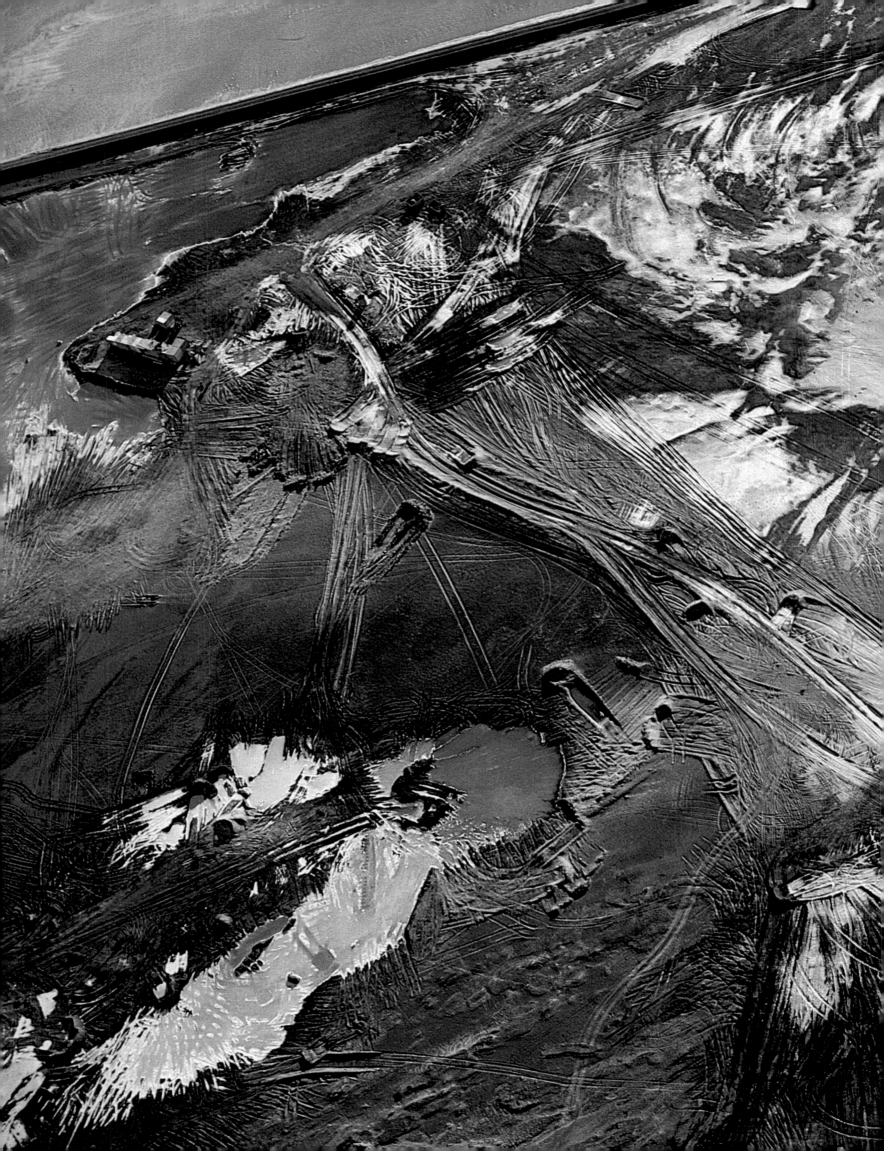

259. Salt crystals being scraped from the rose-coloured brine of an evaporating pan.
260. Flamingoes feed on tiny crustaceans that multiply in their millions in the saline waters of an evaporating pan.
261. Hillocks of brilliant white salt.

THE GERMAN INFLUENCE

Windhoek, capital of Namibia, is a singular and impressive city. Resting in a hollow between low hills its setting is African; its architectural and cultural ambience is European; but its ethos is Namibian. And in the synthesis of these three elements Windhoek in many ways reflects the cosmopolitanism of the country – a unique blend of black, of white, of brown with a distinctly German atmosphere.

Wherever one goes in Namibia the German influence can be felt, seen, heard. Two women on Windhoek's Kaiserstrasse laugh together. One is in the splendid attire of a Herero matron, the other wears western dress and as their laughter subsides and they begin once more to talk you realise that they are speaking German. Yet the German influence reaches far beyond the conversation of two black women on a modern city street: it pervades every aspect of life in the country, be it a board meeting of a mining company, a cattle ranch on the fertile Khomas Hochland, a shop dealing in semi-precious stones, or the menu at a restaurant.

Less than a hundred years have passed since Germany's interest in this land became recognised. But it would be false to assume that before this there was no German – or white – presence in the Transgariep – the land across the Gariep (Orange) River. Missionaries and hunters, traders and explorers, had sought souls and trophies, hides and rare botanical specimens. They had come from Sweden and from the Cape of Good Hope, from England and not least from Germany, and the majority of these men had come with a personal mission.

During the three centuries since Bartholomew Diaz had erected his padrão (cross) at Angra Pequena, now Luderitz Bay, the great powers had found little to attract them along the Benguella Coast. Rumours of gold, copper and of African tribes with huge herds of cattle in the interior had led to some vain attempts to find them. The desert coastline seemed impenetrable; but the sea teemed with whales and seals and shoals of fish, and the offshore islands were rich with guano; so first the Dutch and then the British established settlements at Walvis Bay and Swakopmund. As early as 1795 Britain had hoisted her flag at all the landing-places along the west coast as far north as Angola thus claiming the right to hunt and fish off the coast.

Yet the rumours of gold, copper and cattle-rich tribes persisted. During the 18th century several overland expeditions struggled to the Transgariep; but at the turn of the 19th century no white man had explored further north than the Swakop River.

However, as elsewhere in Africa, it was ultimately the missionaries who opened up the territory. By 1799 the London Missionary Society had established a mission station at Cape Town but it could not meet the demand for missionaries throughout southern Africa. In Berlin, Pastor Jäniche was also training missionaries who were sent out under the auspices of the London office, and so it came to be that the first missionaries in the Transgariep were Germans.

The Albrecht brothers established stations around Warmbad and the Orange River. They built the first brick house in the territory, established the first garden and even had a piano brought out across the desert. They were also first to provide detailed information on the various Nama tribes. Warring tribal factions hindered their work, and eventually they departed, disillusioned. Others arrived, travelling and working under extremely difficult conditions, some to lose their lives; others like Heinrich Schmelen who established a mission station at Bethanie, were more successful.

In 1840, the London Missionary Society ran short of funds and transferred its rights in the territory to the German Rhenish Missionary Society, which sent out Hugo Hahn and Heinrich Kleinschmidt among others. While not always particularly successful in winning converts many of these men won the confidence of the local people, and their stations were regarded as places of refuge in the conflicts between Herero and Nama which dominated the history of the territory for most of the 19th century. They taught basic farming methods, and in times of drought they starved with the tribes. Their true mission was handicapped by traders plying the local people with brandy and firearms in exchange for cattle. And all the while these missionaries introduced the German language, and established the base for later German occupation.

The Berlin Conference convened in 1884 to formulate a blueprint for the carving up of most of the African continent; to ensure that no one stole too large a portion of the prize and to ensure that the delicate balance of power in Europe did not weigh too heavily on any side. And 1884 is an appropriate date from which to trace the expansion of German interest in this wild and forbidding land. Britain was then mistress of a great Empire that straddled vast tracts of Africa, Leopold, King of the Belgians, was exploiting the immense wealth of the Congo Basin, Italy was on the Red Sea and Frenchmen were enjoying the heady scent of Tunisian orange groves. In the newly-united state of Germany, Bismarck too was under pressure to expand German influence. Moreover, in what was to become German South West Africa there were already German nationals who demanded protection.

Bismarck, pragmatic as always and with a parliamentary election ahead, was not motivated by visions of saving souls or piles of African trophies. 'The whole colonial business is a swindle,' he said, 'but we need it for the election.' And so Germany began her involvement with the land behind the Namib Desert; in addition to Togoland, the Cameroons, and German South East Africa (Tanganyika).

In August 1884 she declared the area surrounding Luderitz Bay a Protectorate: by 1886 the northern boundary had been negotiated with Portugal: Britain had declared Bechuanaland (Botswana) a Protectorate and in 1890, in return for German recognition of her interests in Egypt, she negotiated the eastern boundary of German South West Africa.

On the face of it Germany's pickings along the Benguella Coast were meagre. Moreover, Walvis Bay, the seat of what little economic activity there was in the country had already been annexed by Britain in 1878.

It would be some 15 years before German officialdom began to assert power over its new possession. But the land had already captured the imagination of German pioneers imbued with a sense of adventure and no small measure of romanticism. Even in Windhoek today one senses the spirit of these men. Perched above the city are three mediaeval castles typical of the Rhinelands. They were not built for defence but simply as an expression of the mentality of their builders: Old Germany transplanted under the African sun.

Perhaps the most remarkable romantic among these men was Adolf Luderitz. In his youth he had spent time in the tobacco lands of Virginia and Kentucky where he noted with admiration how Britain through her colonies had not only extended her markets but had created havens of refuge for people displaced by industrial growth in Europe. The increasingly industrialized Germany had no colonies at this point.

Although only in 1884 would Africa be officially

262. The Lutheran Church in Windhoek is a landmark that reflects something of two European influences on the territory: the Christian missionaries who helped open up the country, and the Germans who have made it their home.
263, 264. Modern architecture now dominates Windhoek's skyline while within the city the thrust of new development overshadows buildings of an earlier, more romantic, era.

'distributed' among the European powers, Luderitz was well aware that in reality little space remained unclaimed on the map of Africa and he took it upon himself to stake a claim on the behalf of his fatherland. Accordingly, in 1883 he sent a small brig to Angra Pequena and purchased from the Nama Chief of Bethanie, Josef Fredericks, the bay and a radius of five miles inland for £100 and 200 rifles.

The German flag was hoisted – to the accompaniment of non-commital noises from Berlin. But Luderitz was not a man to be deterred by this apparent lack of support. Two months later he bought the whole coastal area from the Orange River to 26⁰ S and 20 miles inland for £500 and 60 rifles.

The British at the Cape watched with concern. British control of Walvis Bay, the only harbour along the entire coast, ensured her hold over whatever economic activity there was in the territory. They had ignored requests to intervene in local affairs and conflicts for they saw no point in being encumbered with additional responsibilities.

But Cecil John Rhodes, that entrepreneur of colonial enterprise, responded to Luderitz's actions by arranging for a British warship to be sent to Walvis Bay to protect her interests. The resulting diplomatic flurry led directly to Germany proclaiming 'Luderitzland' a Protectorate. And so Luderitz's desire for official recognition was at last fulfilled. But his dream of contributing vast wealth to her coffers eluded him. He sent prospectors unsuccessfully to look for copper. Little did they realize they were literally walking on diamonds. Luderitz continued to pour money into similar ventures but he never lived to see any results for whilst out on a prospecting expedition he disappeared, a mystery unexplained to this day.

It was evident that mere romanticism and sunshine were not in themselves sufficient to colonise a land. Bismarck had hoped to leave colonization to private enterprise and accordingly had wasted little expense on administration: he sent out only three officials to take over Germany's new possession. Inevitably they could do nothing more than try to induce the warring Nama and Herero to live peaceably together. When Justice Dr Heinrich Goering attempted to assert some control over the situation by banning the import of alcohol, weapons and ammuniton, he incurred the wrath of both black and white and was forced to seek protection in the British enclave at Walvis Bay. It was clear that without troops, Germany would achieve nothing and at last she agreed to act.

In 1899 Captain Curt von François was sent out and with him came the first official settlers and troops. At Windhoek he built a fort, today known as the Alte Feste, and set out to make Germany's presence felt. The new colonists struggled at first to come to grips with this inhospitable land, its droughts, its floods, its stock diseases. Meanwhile Bismarck still clung to the contention that the development of the country should lie largely in the hands of private companies and Germans were therefore awarded large mining and land concessions.

Administering the local peoples remained a problem. The long-standing enmity between Herero and Nama was further complicated by a new fear, shared by both, of German encroachment on precious resources such as grazing and water. Meanwhile traders aggravated the already volatile situation by enmeshing the indigenous people in debt and providing them with liquor and firearms.

In 1903 the Bondelswarts at Warmbad rose in insurrection against the Germans and the Herero also took this opportunity to settle old scores. With very few exceptions women and children were unharmed but 123 Germans were killed, their farmhouses plundered and burnt, their cattle seized. Reacting with immediate force, troops were sent from Germany commanded by Lieutenant-General Lothar von Trotha. With ruthless efficiency he swept into Namibia and proceeded to subjugate both Nama and Herero in perhaps the bloodiest war of the subcontinent.

The Nama population was reduced by half and they were never to recover their former political identity. The Herero who managed to survive the battle of 11 August 1904, fled through the sandveld to what is now Botswana. Very few survived thirst and starvation. Some 75% of the Herero population perished and all their land and cattle were lost.

In 1908 a final Nama uprising was quelled and the country entered a period of peace and burgeoning prosperity.

By 1914 the white population of Namibia, including troops, numbered no more than 20 000, yet there was remarkable development. German persistence, imagination and hard work were beginning to overcome the natural obstacles of this desert land. Since Walvis Bay was still English, the Germans built a jetty at Swakopmund as an alternative outlet to the sea. A railway was built linking Swakopmund and the centre of administration, Windhoek, which was by the turn of the century connected to Germany by telegraph. Immense mineral deposits were being discovered and Luderitz's dreams of the previous century were becoming realities. Diamonds were found near Luderitz Bay and for the first time the new colony was in a position to pay its way. Swakopmund, Luderitz and Windhoek grew and flourished and everywhere Germans left their mark not only on the economy but on the culture of the country.

Politically, however, the country seemed destined to have her affairs settled for her by those in Europe. The decision to colonise her was taken in Berlin. The event that led to the end of German colonization was also decided in Berlin – the outbreak of World War I led to fears that South West would be used as a strategic base in the Southern Atlantic. It was decided that South African troops under General Louis Botha would prevent this on Britain's behalf. The Germans were defeated and with the Peace of Khorab in 1915, the South African Government established an interim military government. The Treaty of Versailles in 1919 required Germany to surrender all her colonies to the Allies and South West Africa was in 1920 entrusted to South Africa as a mandate by the League of Nations.

But German interest in South West Africa did not end in 1914. Between the two World Wars there was an influx of German nationals into the territory. Many of those who had fled in 1914, returned. Others came to escape from Hitler's attention. Thus in 1945 there were nearly 50 000 whites in South West Africa, by 1970 nearly 100 000. There has also been an influx of South Africans into the area: farmers, businessmen as well as government officials. But the South African Government, as far back as 1920, undertook to respect the language rights of the Germans and today Namibia is officially tri-lingual. Although German can be heard everywhere it is a German peppered in its colloquial form with words derived from English, Afrikaans and indigenous languages. It is a German with a distinctly local flavour.

Today Namibians are on the brink of deciding their own future, and among them are many people of German descent. But they no longer look to Germany as their fatherland. For together with its other inhabitants the destiny of Namibia and not that of Germany, will determine the course of their lives.